Mazal Dabush

THE ALMOND BLOSSOM

CAKES AND BAKING
FROM BLANCHED ALMOND FLOUR...
HIGH PROTEIN – HIGH FIBER – NO TRANS-FATS
GLUTEN-FREE – GUILT FREE!!!

Mazal has been doing my hair and feeding me for years. I don't know what I look forward to more.... my hair or the delicious cakes she brings me! I encouraged her to write her recipes for all to share. So I am so excited she has done that. Her cakes are as healthy as they are beautiful. They look as good as they are nutricious. Thanks Mazal

Love, Sari

I have been catering for 25 years and I recently had an opportunity to taste many of Mazal's baked goods. What a delicious collection of flavors, one better than the next. I have used some of her cakes and cookies in my business for high end clients receiving rave reviews. Try some of these recipes. They are simply scrumptious!!
Shirlie Burgudy Creek Catering

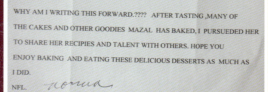

Why am I writing this forward.???? After tasting, many of the cakes and other goodies Mazal has baked, I pursueded her to share her recipies and talent with others. Hope you enjoy baking and eating these delicious desserts as much as I did.
NFL. Norma

I have been in search of good-tasting baked goods that are gluten free and was delighted to discover Mazel's array of delicious cakes and cookies. Her almond cake and chocolate poppyseed cake are my favorites.
- Anne Reilly

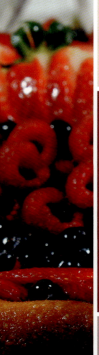

Mazals desserts are the best I have had - and a true piece of art
Brenda

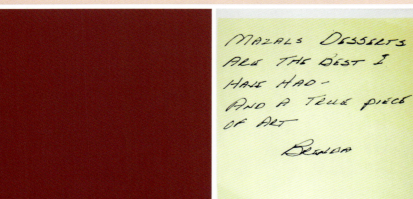

This is a great way to enjoy really tasty desserts without feeling guilty. Whether you have medical conditions or just want to eat healthy but don't want to give up desserts, you will love this book. This has a great collection of recipes which are flour free, high in protein, easy to follow, easy to make and ingredients which aren't hard to find. These recipes are just as delicious as they are beautiful! A real masterpiece and a must have for every cook.

Judge Susan M. Speer
Los Angeles, California

Our grandma's cakes are the perfect guilt-free breakfast, dessert, or late night snack! It's amazing how something so healthy can taste so good! Everytime she spoils us with her cakes, they are all gone in under an hour. It is so hard to choose just one favorite cake or cookie because they are all so good! These cakes make staying healthy and in shape easy.

We hope you ♡ our grandma's cakes just as much as we do!

Love,
Nurelle, Karyn, & Adam

Mazal's Almond Cake is amazing!! It's super moist and taste so rich you would think it was pure fat! But it's totally healthy!! No flour or sugar! Thanks Mazal!!
— Dawn Whitesell

EVERYTHING IS SO DELICIOUS AND LOOKS SO APPETIZING BEST OF ALL SO HEALTHY!
KATHARINA

I want to eat Mazal's Cakes every day!
— Davis Alexander
Recipe Tester

BSD

This book grew out of repeated attempts to create scrumptious and healthful cookies and cakes for myself and anyone searching for satisfying desserts without the harm or guilt.

After developing recipes with many types of gluten-free flour, I discovered high-protein, blanched almond flour. It's delicate nutty flavor is superior to anything I'd worked with, and its nutritional value far surpasses wheat flour.

I invite you to enjoy these creative, easy-to-prepare recipes in all their variations.

I am happy to share these with you and hope that you will enjoy these unique, rich in protein, easy-to-make recipes.

From my heart to yours,

Mazal Dabush

©
ALL RIGHTS RESERVED BY MAZAL DABUSH 2019

No parts of this book and in its hebrew version "PRICHAT HASHAKED", neither pictures nor text,
may be copied or reproduced in any form, paper or electronic,
without the expressed written consent of the author.
mazaldabush5@gmail.com

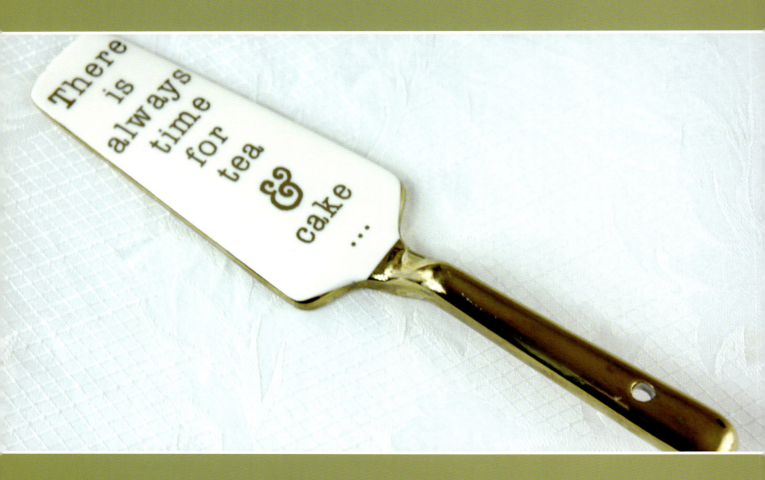

Measuring: All the recipes in the book call for imperial measuring cups and spoons.

Baking Pans: Pan size is recommended for each recipe; however, your choice of pan or muffin pan can be used by adjusting baking time.

Passover: Recipes may be adapt Passover with the exception of pages: 92, 94, 96, 112 and 114. To bake these cakes and cookies for Passover, please see Mazal Secret's for substitutions indicated by a ⓟ.

Flours: For recipes that call for "blanched almond flour", do not substitute with other flours. For recipes calling for "gluten-free all purpose" flour, rice flour, potato starch flour or Teff flour can be substituted.

Allergies: Please be mindful of seeds and legumes included in my recipes to which you may be allergic

Thank you **G-od** from whom all is given...

To my husband, **Victor** -- the one who supports my every step.

To my children **Emily Mally, Avishai, Jonathan**, my son-in-law, **Israel Ulik** and my grandchildren **Nurelle, Karyn** and **Adam** – for their appreciation of these recipes

To **my mother and siblings** – for always encouraging me to experiment.

To **my mother-in-law, OB"M** – from whom I learned the finer points of baking.

To **my friends & clients--** who have enjoyed and taste-tested my recipes throughout the year

And a special thanks to my son, **Avishai**, for taking the beautiful photographs in this book.

To **Hasida** for translating this book from Hebrew to English

To **Sari Drucker** who helped and encouraged me for years

To **A.L Baruch, Davis Alexander, and Anne Reilly** for their editing help

To **Chani Sebag** for her overall design of the book.

{Table of Contents}

Mazal's Secrets

Throughout this book, you will find tips and advice that I am happy to share with you to make your baking experience fun and easy. The tips appear on specific recipe pages but can be used for all recipes in general. As fast as the almond tree blossoms, throughout Mazal's Secrets you'll find that new recipe ideas will blossom.

Cakes

- Almond Cake 14
- Almond Mousse Cake, Marzipan-Flavored 16
- Nut Mousse Cake Variety 18
- Pecan Cake 20
- Mixed Nuts and Chocolate Cake ... 22
- Walnut Cake 24
- Blueberry Honey Cake 26
- Lemon Cake 28
- Cooked Quinoa and Pineapple Cake 30
- Honey Cake 32
- Moist Honey-Orange Cake (or Coffee) 34
- Pumpkin Cake with Fresh Dates 36
- Honey Cake with Pears 38
- Apple Cake 40
- Dried and Fresh Fruit Cake 42
- Orange Cake 44
- Almond Blossom Cake 46
- More Additions and Upgrades for Almond Blossom Cake 48
- Additions and Upgrades 50
- Cold Tofutti Cheesecake 54
- Chocolate Marble Cake 58
- Banana Pecan Bread 60
- Poppy Snow Cake 62
- Poppy Seed and Tofu Cheesecake 64
- Tofu Cheesecake with Berries 66
- Topping Options 68
- Basic Pie Preparation 70
- Basic Pie Fillings 74
- Pumpkin Pie Cheesecake 76

Cookies

- Tahini cookies 80
- Manna Cookies 82
- Manna Basic Cookies (filling) 84
- Basic Manna Cookies 86
- Pumpkin seed Cookies 88

- Sesame Tahini Cookies 90
- Peanut Butter Oat Cookies 92
- Granola-Sesame Cookies 94
- Oatmeal-Chia Cookies 96
- Biscotti 98
- Almond Cookies 100

Unique Treats

- Vegan Energy Bars (No-bake) 104
- Marzipan 106
- Chocolate Tahini Sweets 108
- Homemade Almond Milk 110
- Ginger Energy Bar 112
- Vegan Energy Bars (No-bake) 114
- Baked Stuffed Apples 116
- Baked Almond Pancake 118

Muffins

- Apple Muffin 122
- Flax Seed and Cooked Quinoa Muffin 124
- Carrot and Pineapple Muffin 126
- Banana Muffin 128
- Zucchini Muffin 130

Savory

- Almond Bread 134
- Miracle Bread 136
- Almond Savory Bagels, ... 138
- Vegetable Tofu Quiche 140

"Healthful and Delicious Baked Goods for the Heart and Soul

I was born in Israel in 1955 and, as a child, I had a sweet tooth. At the age of 12, I discovered baking. I loved the creativity inherent in baking, and, not surprisingly, I enjoyed indulging in the treats I baked. I was encouraged by my family who appreciated my skill; but the combination of my tastes and talent led to out-of-control eating! Cakes and cookies became an addiction and resulted in weight gain. This led me to research health and nutrition, and, after studying the writings of Maimonides (the Rambam), I learned to honor my health and soul to control my eating. I learned to eat for nourishment, not for desire and I made the decision to give up white flour.

The change came for me in my 30s, when I moved to America. For me, it was a long and difficult path to healthful eating. The recipes I developed along the way helped me replace harmful ingredients with nourishing substitutes that satisfied me. And they can be enjoyed completely-- because they are deeply delicious, filling and leave you feeling good, not guilty.

Today I bake only with ingredients that are natural, healthful and nourishing. I use no artificial or processed ingredients. There are no trans-fats, highly- processed sugars or artery-clogging margarine in my recipes; and most of my cakes have no oil added. When adding oil in other recipes, I use raw tahini, coconut oil, olive oil, and canola oil. I mostly use almond and whole nut flours, unroasted nuts and seeds that add protein, flavor and nutritional value. I have also eliminated addictive and poisonous artificial sweeteners that harm our bodies and the growing bodies of our children. My creations are free of the side effects that come along with eating gluten, overly-processed sugars, artificial ingredients and trans-fats.

After every successful baking creation, I quickly write down the recipe. This is how the recipes in this book were collected and tasted by my family, friends and my many clients in my hairdressing business.

Sharing these tastes and tips led to constructive dialogues with women who offered suggestions and evaluations. I am overjoyed that I can teach, learn and share my creations.

I hope you enjoy baking these recipes as much as I have enjoyed and benefited from creating them.

Dedication to G-d

I thank G-d for this incredible gift, the ability to create through years of trial, error and experience.

After every successful baking creation, I am quick to write down the recipe.

This is how the recipes in this book were collected and tasted by my family, friends and my many clients (I am a hairdresser living in Los Angeles).

Many women who have tasted these creations offered suggestions and compliments, which I was always receptive to. They have always encouraged me to share my creations and I am overjoyed that I can now teach others.

I would like to include some words of wisdom that I have learned from King David (on whom should be peace) in Psalms which reads "Learn, Teach, Save, Do and Keep":

Learn- I learned the nutritional value and advantages of almonds and was persistent during many challenging attempts to learn the 'ins' and 'outs' of baking with almond flour.

Teach- From this learning experience I love sharing with my family and community the ability to enjoy baked goods without guilt.

Save- I attempt to control myself and to refrain from consuming ingredients that are harmful to my body and soul.

Do- I decided to be diligent about these principles on a daily basis and to implement these eating practices for the benefit of myself, my family and my community.

And Keep- I teach you these recipes with great love, eager for you to receive the health benefits that I have, and in this way, I keep the commandment "Love your neighbor as you love yourself."

Many thanks and wishing success to all!

Mazal

Almonds are considered to have magical healing powers

❝ Various research suggests the consumption of 24-32 almonds daily. The raw almond is gluten-free and has beneficial probiotic effects. Almonds are rich in vitamins, minerals, protein, and fibers which also assist in weight loss. Even the almond fat is a healthy fat that sustains the body for a longer time. When compared with other fats, the calorie count is more or less the same ,but almonds are cholesterol-free and low in saturated fat. The almond can also strengthen the muscles, and balance insulin to reduce sugar craving. Almonds are filled with antioxidants.

They are good for the heart, depression, stress, and help prevent wrinkles. Almonds could also strengthen teeth, hair, and nails. You'll find that almond cakes have more protein and less carbs compared to other cakes.

The secret to my healthful baking is: More protein, fewer carbohydrates If you crave a slice of cake or another sweet treat, eat one that fills you up, guilt-free! ❞

Turbinado Sugar

❝ Turbinado sugar is a slightly coarse, light brown sugar obtained from the first pressing of sugar cane, and gets its name from the turbines used to process it. It is ideal for vegetarians and vegans because it is not processed with bone char, which is used to create the white color of highly refined sugar. A single teaspoon of turbinado sugar contains 20 calories, of which 5 grams are complex carbohydrates. Turbinado sugar also contains trace elements of beneficial minerals, which white sugar does not. ❞

Cakes

Cakes & Almonds

14 — 15

Mazal's Secrets

- Avoiding parchment paper is ok, but don't forget to spray the pan.
- This is a basic cake; you can add chia seeds, nuts and other ingredients.
- Mixing gluten-free flours such as potato flour and rice flour and/or tapioca flour works well, too.
- Adding a half cup fresh applesauce or orange juice.

Almond Cake

~ A cake full of flavor, health and love ~

Ingredients

9 large eggs
Pinch of sea salt
1 tablespoon freshly squeezed lemon juice
1 ¼ cups turbinado sugar
2 ½ cups finely ground almonds grind in food processor or almond meal
¼ cup gluten-free all purpose flour or potato flour
2 tablespoon ground flax seeds
½ teaspoon vanilla extract
1 tablespoon baking powder
1 tablespoon finely grated lemon zest

Streusel Topping

½ cup sliced almonds
1 tablespoon turbinado sugar
¼ teaspoon cinnamon

10" round springform cake pan
16 servings
About 190 calorie per serving

Method:

1.
Preheat oven to 350 degrees F. Place oven rack in middle of oven. Fit a parchment round cut-to-size into bottom of springform pan. Spray parchment and sides of springform lightly with cooking spray.

2.
In a mixer, whip egg whites with salt and lemon juice. Add sugar slowly, whip to stiff peaks.

3.
In a separate bowl, whisk the egg yolks until slightly foamy. Gently fold in the beaten egg white mixture, making sure the mixture stays well aerated. Add all other ingredients.

4.
Whisk the almond flour with the gluten-free flour in a medium bowl. Using a silicone spatula gradually fold the flour mixture to the egg mixture to obtain a unified mixture.

5.
Pour the batter into prepared pan. Mix the streusel topping: sliced almond, turbinado sugar and cinnamon and sprinkle over the top of the cake.

6.
Bake in preheated oven approximately 30 minutes until color is light golden brown. Insert toothpick between center and edge comes out clean. Remove from oven and move to rack to cool.

For a smaller cake, use a 6 inch springform pan, and these amounts; then proceed with above directions.

Ingredients

6 large eggs
¾ cup turbinado sugar
1 ½ cup almond meal
⅓ cup gluten-free all purpose flour
And add the rest of ingredients...

BLANCHED ALMOND FLOUR AND ALMOND MEAL

Blanched almond flour is ground from almonds that have been plunged in boiling water to remove their skins. It is finely ground.

Almond meal is ground from whole almonds that still have their skins on. The result is slightly coarser than blanched almond flour.

Only substitute one for the other as directed in my recipes, or the resulting color and texture of your cake will be different than indicated.

Cakes & Almonds

Almond Mousse Cake, Marzipan-Flavored

8" round or square baking pan
12 servings
About 125 calories per serving for chocolate mousse
About 160 calories per serving for whip cream mousse cake

Ingredients:

6 large eggs
Pinch of sea salt
2 tablespoons freshly squeezed lemon juice
½ cup turbinado sugar
7 oz. (200g) 60% dark chocolate bar
1 cup blanched almond flour (or almond meal)
¼ cup freshly squeezed orange juice or ½ cup Tofutti sour cream

(1) For Marzipan flavor: (for marzipan decoration refer to secret).
1 teaspoon almond extract
(2) For Raspberry cake:
1 cup raspberries
(optional: replace the almond extract with whiskey or rum extract)
Garnish with whip cream and raspberries
(3) For whip cream cake:
1 cup Rich Whip Liquid ready to whip cream
Garnish with ½ cup chopped hazelnuts

Method:

1.
Preheat oven to 350 degrees F. Place oven rack in middle of oven. Fit a parchment round cut-to-size into bottom of springform pan. Spray parchment and sides of springform lightly with cooking spray.

2.
Break the chocolate into small pieces. Put chocolate and orange juice in skillet over medium low heat. Stir occasionally until melted. Take off heat immediately so it won't burn.

3.
In a mixer, whip egg whites with salt and lemon juice. Add sugar slowly, whip to stiff peaks.

4.
In a separate bowl, whisk the egg yolks until slightly foamy. Gently fold in the beaten egg white mixture, making sure the mixture stays well aerated.

5.
Continue to add the melted chocolate to the batter with a gentle fold.

6.
Whisk the almond flour in a medium bowl. Using a silicone spatula gradually fold the flour mixture to the egg mixture to obtain a unified mixture.

7.
Put aside about ½ cup of the batter for the top coating (or more if desired). Add almond extract to batter for marzipan flavor, or optional: add whiskey or rum extract for other two cakes.
For raspberry cake spread 1 cup raspberry and press into batter.

8.
Pour the batter into prepared pan. Bake in preheated oven approximately 25 minutes. Insert toothpick between center and edge comes out clean. Remove from oven and move to rack to cool.
For whip cream cake: Spread whipped cream over cake using a spatula before chocolate coating.

9.
Using a spatula spread the chocolate coating on top of the cake.
Refer to cakes above to garnish accordingly.

Mazal's Secrets

- **For a rich tasting Almond Mousse Marzipan Cake,** prepare marzipan ahead of time, refer to marzipan recipe, roll marzipan into desired shape and decorate on top of the chocolate cream.

- **For Banana Chocolate Mousse Cake,** add 1 medium ripe banana while mixing egg yolk, to give the cake a special aroma and taste.

- **To make Brownie Cake** don't set any ingredients aside, mix all ingredients into Brownie Cake.

- **For a fuller, richer consistency,** add ½ cup of chopped dark chocolate to the batter.

Same lady, different outfit...

Cakes & Almonds

Nut Mousse Cake Variety

~ My grandchildren love this cake and request it for dessert at every Friday night dinner. ~

8" round or square baking pan
12 servings
About 125 calories per serving for chocolate mousse
About 160 calories per serving for whip cream mousse cake

Ingredients:
6 large eggs
Pinch of sea salt
2 tablespoons freshly squeezed lemon juice
½ cup turbinado sugar
¼ cup almond milk or freshly squeezed orange juice
1 teaspoon whiskey, rum, or vanilla extract (optional)
7oz (200 gr) Dark chocolate

Options:

(1) Mousse Walnut Cake
1 cup finely ground walnuts
For decoration: ½ cup halved walnuts.

(2) Mousse Pecan Cake
1 cup finely ground pecans
For decoration: ½ cup pecans

(3) Mousse Coconut Cake
¾ cup unsweetened desiccated/ground coconut
½ blanched almond flour (or finely ground walnuts)
For decoration: ¼ cup desiccated/ground coconut

Method:

1.
Preheat oven to 350 degrees F. Place oven rack in middle of oven. Fit a parchment round cut-to-size into bottom of springform pan. Spray parchment and sides of springform lightly with cooking spray.

2.
Break the chocolate into small pieces. Put chocolate and orange juice in skillet over medium low heat. Stir occasionally until melted. Take off heat immediately so it won't burn.

3.
In a mixer, whip egg whites with salt and lemon juice. Add sugar slowly, whip to stiff peaks.

4.
In a separate bowl, whisk the egg yolks until slightly foamy. Gently fold in the beaten egg white mixture, making sure the mixture stays well aerated.

5.
Add the melted chocolate to the batter with a gentle fold using a silicone spatula. Add optional whiskey, rum or vanilla extract to batter set aside.

6.
Add the remaining ingredients from the desired cake above (1) - (3) to the batter. Gently and slowly fold the batter to obtain a unified mixture. Put aside about ½ cup of the batter for the top coating (or more if desired).

7.
Pour into prepared pan. Bake in preheated oven approximately 25 minutes. Insert toothpick between center and edge comes out clean. Remove from oven and move to rack to cool.

8.
Using a spatula spread the chocolate coating on top of the cake. Garnish desired cake accordingly.

Mazal's Secrets

- Add flavor with a few drops rum, almond extract or bourbon to the chocolate.
In order for the cake to cool properly, and not continue to bake in the hot pan, you must cool it on a wire cooling rack so that air can circulate underneath the hot pan and cool it off.

- Using cane sugar, xylitol, stevia, or truvia works too.

Cakes & Almonds

Mazal's Secrets

- To decorate the cake: mix 1 tablespoon coarse turbinado sugar, cinnamon, and some gluten-free oats. Adds crispiness.

- Interchange the pecans with hazelnuts.

- Interchange the rice flour with potato or any gluten-free flour.

Pecan Cake

~ A cake rich in protein that is satisfying and delicious! ~

10" round baking pan
16 servings
About 220 calories per serving

Ingredients:

9 large eggs
Pinch of sea salt
2 teaspoons freshly squeezed lemon juice
1¼ cups turbinado sugar
1 tablespoon of vanilla sugar or ½ teaspoon of vanilla extract
2 ¼ cups finely ground pecans
2 heaping tablespoons rice or quinoa flour
½ cup freshly squeezed orange juice
zest of a medium size orange
zest of half a lemon
1 tablespoon baking powder
¼ cup coarsely chopped pecans
2 tablespoon ground flaxseed
2 tablespoon chia seeds

Streusel Topping:
About 20 pecan halves
1 tablespoon turbinado sugar
½ teaspoon cinnamon

Method:

1.
Preheat oven to 350 degrees F. Place oven rack in middle of oven. Fit a parchment round cut-to-size into bottom of springform pan. Spray parchment and sides of springform lightly with cooking spray.

2.
In a mixer, whip egg whites with salt and lemon juice. Add sugar slowly, whip to stiff peaks.

3.
In a separate bowl, whisk the egg yolks until slightly foamy. Gently fold in the beaten egg white mixture, making sure the mixture stays well aerated. Add the orange juice and the vanilla.

4.
In a medium bowl, whisk the raw ground pecan with the quinoa flour. Using a silicone spatula gradually fold the flour mixture to the egg mixture to obtain a unified mixture. Add ¼ cup chopped pecans to the batter. Add all other ingredients and mix well.

5.
Pour into prepared pan. In a separate small bowl mix 1 tablespoon turbinado sugar with ½ teaspoon cinnamon. Spread the mix over the cake batter. Place pecan halves over batter.

6.
Bake in preheated oven approximately 30 minutes until light golden brown. Insert toothpick between center and edge comes out clean.

Cakes & Almonds

Mixed Nuts and Chocolate Cake

~ An assorted cake that leaves a lingering taste- cover photo ~

10" round baking pan
16 servings
About 212 per serving

Ingredients:

9 large eggs
Pinch of sea salt
2 tablespoons freshly squeezed lemon juice
1¼ cups turbinado sugar
2¼ cups medium/fine ground nuts (pecans, walnuts, almonds)
½ cup chopped 60% dark chocolate bar
¼ cup quinoa or gluten-free all purpose flour
¼ cup mixture of ground flax and chia seeds
½ teaspoon vanilla extract
½ teaspoon finely grated lemon zest
1 tablespoon baking powder

Streusel Topping:
¼ cup sliced almonds mix with ¼ coarsely chopped walnuts
2 tablespoons coarsely chopped chocolate
1 tablespoon turbinado sugar
½ teaspoon cinnamon

Mazal's Secrets

- My preference for using more almond flour and nuts is because they are higher in protein and omega 3 to leave you fully satisfied without leaving you craving and addicted to sugars, compared with other gluten-free flours that are higher in carbs.

- To finely zest the rind of a lemon, use the smallest holes on your box grater, or, better yet, use a microplane, which is made for grating citrus zest.

Method:

1.
Preheat oven to 350 degrees F. Place oven rack in middle of oven. Fit a parchment round cut-to-size into bottom of springform pan. Spray parchment and sides of springform lightly with cooking spray.

2.
In a mixer, whip egg whites with salt and lemon juice. Add sugar slowly, whip to stiff peaks..

3.
In a separate bowl, whisk the egg yolks until slightly foamy. Using a spatula gently fold in the beaten egg white mixture, making sure the mixture stays well aerated. Continue to gradually fold in chopped chocolate, ground nuts, quinoa flour, flax seeds/chia seeds, lemon zest, and baking powder to obtain a unified mixture.

4.
Pour into prepared pan. In a separate small bowl mix streusel topping and sprinkle on top of the batter.

5.
Bake in preheated oven approximately 30 minutes until color is light golden brown. Insert toothpick between center and edge comes out clean. Remove from oven and move to rack to cool.

cover photo

Cakes & Almonds

Mazal's Secrets

- Create a **rich whipped cream cake**, bake a third of the batter; coat with raspberry jam or chocolate cream combined with whisky extract, spread whip cream on top, and decorate with fruit, nuts, or chocolate. The remaining batter, make muffins!

- Turbinado sugar could be reduced to 1 cup

- Adding a mixture of chia and flax seeds works for all cakes!

Walnut Cake

~ This is THE cake to choose for high protein and fiber ~

10" round baking pan
16 servings
About 205 calories per serving

Ingredients:

9 large eggs
Pinch of sea salt
2 tablespoons freshly squeezed lemon juice
1¼ cups turbinado sugar
2 cups medium fine ground walnuts
½ cup quinoa flour or gluten-free all purpose flour
1 teaspoon vanilla extract
½ teaspoon finely grated lemon zest
1 tablespoon baking powder

Method:

1.
Preheat oven to 350 degrees F. Place oven rack in middle of oven. Fit a parchment round cut-to-size into bottom of springform pan. Spray parchment and sides of springform lightly with cooking spray.

2.
In a mixer, whip egg whites with salt and lemon juice. Add sugar slowly, whip to stiff peaks..

3.
In a separate bowl, whisk the egg yolks until slightly foamy. Using a silicone spatula gently fold in the beaten egg white mixture, making sure the mixture stays well aerated. Continue to gradually fold in ground walnuts, flour, vanilla extract, lemon zest, and baking powder to obtain a unified mixture.

4.
Pour into prepared pan. Sprinkle walnuts evenly over the cake mixture.

5.
Bake in preheated oven approximately 30 minutes until color is light golden brown. Insert toothpick between center and edge comes out clean. Remove from oven and move to rack to cool.

Cakes & Almonds

Blueberry Honey Cake

~ A three-in-one mixed berry cake ~

9" round baking pan

12 servings
About 300 calories per serving

Ingredients:

3 large eggs
½ cup honey
¼ cup freshly squeezed orange juice or almond milk
1 tablespoon cinnamon
½ teaspoon baking soda
½ teaspoon vanilla extract
2½ cups blanched almond flour
½ cup dried cranberry
2 cups fresh blueberry (raspberries or cherries)

Method:

1.
Preheat oven to 350 degrees F. Place oven rack in middle of oven. Fit a parchment round cut-to-size into bottom of springform pan. Spray parchment and sides of springform lightly with cooking spray.

2.
In a medium bowl, beat the eggs with a fork. Mix in the honey, orange juice, cinnamon, baking soda, vanilla extract, and dried cranberries. In a separate medium bowl, whisk the flours.

3.
Using a silicone spatula gradually fold the flour mixture to the egg mixture to obtain a unified mixture.

4.
Pour the batter into the prepared pan. Lightly press blueberries on surface of cake.

5.
Bake for approximately 25 minutes in the preheated oven until the color is light golden brown. Insert toothpick between center and edge comes out clean. Remove from oven and move to rack to cool.

Trio cake:
After pouring batter in pan, lightly score surface in thirds. Pour a ¾ cup of raspberry, cherry, or blueberry. Lightly press blueberries in alternate sections of surface.

Mazal's Secrets

- Substitute cherries, raspberries or other berries in season for blueberries.

- Separate the egg white and egg yolk while cold (from refrigerator) for best results. Cover egg white and wait until room temp to whip (to achieve room temp faster place egg white bowl into a warm water bowl).

Cakes & Almonds

Lemon Cake

~ The citrusy aroma provides brightness in winter and refreshment in summer ~

10" round baking pan
16 servings
About 190 calories per serving

Ingredients:
9 large eggs

Pinch of sea salt
¼ cup freshly squeezed lemon juice

1½ cups turbinado sugar
1 large seedless lemon sliced, cooked
1 tablespoon baking powder
1 finely grated lemon peel
1½ teaspoons vanilla extract
2½ cups blanched almond flour
½ cup quinoa or gluten-free all purpose flour

Lemon Tofutti Sour Cream Frosting (optional)
Ingredients:
½ cup water, divided
1 heaping tablespoon cornstarch
¼ cup turbinado sugar
¼ cup Tofutti sour cream
¼ cup freshly squeezed lemon juice
1 tablespoon finely grated lemon zest

Preparation

1. Mix ¼ cup of the water with cornstarch until smooth.

2. In medium saucepan, bring remaining ¼ cup water and sugar to a boil.

3. Add cornstarch mixture to sugar water and return to boil. Lower heat and stir until slightly thickened and smooth.

4. Take off heat and add Tofutti sour cream, lemon juice and zest while stirring and let cool.

5. Spread on cake just before serving.

Can be made ahead of time and keep refrigerated.

Method:

1.
Preheat oven to 350 degrees F. Place oven rack in middle of oven. Spray cooking spray on bundt pan.

2.
In a sauce pan, cook the slices of lemon and 1 tablespoon of turbinado sugar and ¼ cup water just enough to cover the lemons until soften, blend to a sauce.

3.
In a mixer, whip egg whites with salt and lemon juice. Add sugar slowly, whip to stiff peaks.

4.
In a separate bowl, whisk the egg yolks until slightly foamy. Using a silicone spatula gently fold in the beaten egg white mixture, making sure the mixture stays well aerated. Add lemon sauce, lemon peel, baking powder, and vanilla extract.

5.
Whisk the almond flour and quinoa flour in a small bowl and gradually add the flour mixture to the egg mixture to obtain a unified mixture. Pour into prepared pan.

6.
Bake in preheated oven approximately 30 minutes until color is light golden brown. Insert toothpick between center and edge comes out clean. Remove from oven and move to rack to cool.

Mazal's Secrets

- Can make a smaller cake by decreasing the amount of the ingredients by a third.

- Garnish by sifting powdered sugar on top.

Cakes & Almonds

Mazal's Secrets

- Replace the pineapple fruit with any seasonal fruits; such as plums, peaches or apricots.

- Turbinado sugar can be substituted for cane sugar for all the cakes!

Cooked Quinoa and Pineapple Cake

~ A surprisingly delicious combination! ~

10" round or square baking pan
12 servings
About 260 calories per serving

Ingredients:

9 large eggs
Pinch of sea salt
2 tablespoons freshly squeezed lemon juice
¼ cup coconut oil or tahini paste
1 tablespoon vanilla extract
1 ¼ cup turbinado sugar
1 tablespoon baking powder
1 cup fresh chopped pineapple
2 cups cooked quinoa (see quinoa back label)
1 cup blanched almond flour
1 cup quinoa flour
¼ cup dried cranberries

Streusel Topping:
Sliced pineapple
2 tablespoons dried cranberries

Method:

1.
Preheat oven to 350 degrees F. Place oven rack in middle of oven. Fit a parchment round cut-to-size into bottom of springform pan. Spray parchment and sides of springform lightly with cooking spray. Pad the pan with 2 teaspoons of blanched almond flour.

2.
In a mixer, whip egg whites with salt and lemon juice. Add sugar slowly, whip to stiff peaks.

3.
In a separate small bowl, whisk the egg yolks and coconut oil until slightly foamy. Gently fold in the beaten egg white mixture, making sure the mixture stays well aerated.

4.
Whisk the almond flour and quinoa flour in a small bowl. Using a silicone spatula gradually fold the flour mixture to the egg mixture to obtain a unified mixture.

5.
Using a silicone spatula add cooked quinoa and pineapple to the egg mixture.

6.
Pour into prepared pan. Press fruit on top of batter.

7.
Bake in preheated oven approximately 30-40 minutes until color is light golden brown. Insert toothpick between center and edge comes out clean. Remove from oven and move to rack to cool.

Cakes & Almonds

Honey Cake

9" round or square baking pan
16 servings
About 315 calories per serving

Ingredients:

4 extra large eggs
Pinch of sea salt
2 tablespoons freshly squeezed lemon juice
¾ cups turbinado sugar
¾ cup honey
¾ cup strong hot tea (2 bags) mixed with 2 heaping teaspoons instant coffee
½ cup olive oil (or coconut oil)
1 level tablespoon cinnamon
A pinch of cloves
A pinch of ginger
1½ cups blanched almond flour or almond meal
2 cups Teff flour (or quinoa flour)
1 teaspoon baking powder
½ teaspoon baking soda
2 tablespoons applesauce

Streusel Topping:
1 tablespoon turbinado sugar
½ teaspoon cinnamon
⅓ cup of slivered almonds

Mazal's Secrets

- Add chia seeds, flax seeds, raisins, almonds and chopped nuts.

Method:

1. Preheat oven to 350 degrees F. Place oven rack in middle of oven. Fit a parchment round cut-to-size into bottom of springform pan. Spray parchment and sides of springform lightly with cooking spray.

2. Steep 2 tea bags in ¾ cup of hot water and add 2 heaping teaspoons of instant coffee and honey. Let it cool. In a mixer, whip egg whites with salt and lemon juice. Add sugar slowly, whip to stiff peaks.

3. In a separate bowl, whisk the egg yolks until slightly foamy. Gently fold in the beaten egg white mixture, making sure the mixture stays well aerated.

4. Add oil, and applesauce to egg mixture. Add the cooled tea mix.

5. In a separate medium bowl, whisk the quinoa flour with the almond flour. Add cinnamon, cloves, ginger, baking powder, and baking soda. Using a silicone spatula gradually fold the flour mixture to the egg mixture to obtain a unified mixture.

6. Pour unified mixture into prepared pan. Mix the streusel topping: sugar, cinnamon, and slivered almonds and sprinkle on top.

7. Bake in preheated oven approximately 30-40 minutes until color is light golden brown. Insert toothpick between center and edge comes out clean. Remove from oven and move to rack to cool.

~Teff Flour~

Teff flour comes from Ethiopia. It is a high fiber food, that is very filling, and has many health benefits. Various research has shown that teff flour naturally balance hormone levels, boost immunity, and stimulate digestion. The flour has a very rich taste, and could be exchanged for any gluten-free all purpose flour used in the book. The flour would give any cake a darker color, so to keep the cake the color pictured in the book, only substitute teff flour for dark colored cakes.

Cakes & Almonds

Mazal's Secrets

- **For orange-honey cake,** add seasonal fresh fruit.
- It's always good to put baking powder and baking soda near the end.

Moist Honey-Orange Cake (or Coffee)

~ This irresistible cake is moist and delicious... you won't want to stop eating it! ~

9" round baking pan or 9x5" loaf pan
16 servings
About 224 calories per serving

Ingredients:

4 large eggs
Pinch of sea salt
1 tablespoon freshly squeezed lemon juice
¾ cup honey
1 teaspoon vanilla extract
½ teaspoon baking soda
1 level tablespoon cinnamon
2 ½ cups blanched almond flour
2 tablespoons chia seeds (optional)
2 tablespoons ground flax seed (optional)

(1) For Honey-Orange Cake:
(add to the batter)
½ cup freshly squeezed orange juice
2 tablespoons finely grated orange peel

Honey-Orange Cake - Topping
(Before baking)
¼ cup cranberries
¼ cup chopped walnuts (or other nuts)
¼ cup sesame seeds

Orange Syrup Topping Sauce
(After baking while the cake is hot)
2 tablespoons honey mixed with ½ cup freshly squeezed orange juice
(microwave honey to make it more soluble)

(2) For Honey-Coffee Cake:
(Add to the batter)
½ cup of strong black coffee
¼ teaspoon cloves
¼ teaspoon ground ginger
½ cup slivered almonds to scatter on the batter (before baking)

Coffee-Syrup Topping Sauce
(After baking while the cake is hot)
3 tablespoons honey mixed with ¼ cup of hot black coffee

Prepare topping:
- Microwave for about a minute.
- 2 tablespoons of honey add ½ cup of fresh squeezed orange juice.
- (For coffee syrup topping add coffee to the honey)

Method:

1.
Preheat oven to 350 degrees F. Place oven rack in middle of oven. Fit a parchment round cut-to-size into bottom of springform or loaf pan. Spray parchment and sides of springform lightly with cooking spray.

2.
In a medium bowl using a wire whisk beat the whole eggs with salt, honey, vanilla, cinnamon, baking soda, flax seeds and chia seeds.

3.
Whisk blanched almond flour using a silicone spatula gradually fold the flour mixture to the egg mixture to obtain a unified mixture.

Cake 1:
If making the Honey Orange Cake add orange juice and finely grated orange peel to the batter. Pour batter into prepared pan and add cranberries, walnuts, and sesame seeds on top, before baking.

Cake 2:
If making Honey-Coffee cake add black coffee, cloves, and ginger to the batter. Pour batter into prepared pan and add slivered almonds on top, before baking.

4.
Bake in preheated oven approximately 30 minutes until color is light golden brown. Insert toothpick between center and edge comes out clean.

5.
Once baked, while the cake is hot. Poke holes with a thin skewer in the cake. Add Honey Orange Topping sauce to the Honey Orange cake and Honey Coffee Topping sauce to the Honey Coffee cake while hot. Remove from oven and move to rack to cool.

Cakes & Almonds

Pumpkin Cake with Fresh Dates

~ Take advantage of the short fresh date season ~

9" round baking pan
16 servings
About 270 per serving

Ingredients:

4 large eggs
¾ cup turbinado sugar
1 tablespoon vanilla extract
4 tablespoons honey or maple syrup
1½ cups grated fresh pumpkin or banana squash
½ cup pumpkin purée fresh (or canned pumpkin purée)
1 tablespoon baking powder
½ teaspoon baking soda
¼ teaspoon ginger
Pinch of cloves
1 teaspoon cinnamon
2 tablespoon chia seeds
2 tablespoon flax seeds
8 -10 fresh sliced dates
1½ cups blanched almond flour
⅓ cup of quinoa flour or Teff flour

Streusel Topping:
½ cup of fine slivered almonds
4 fresh sliced dates

Method:

1.
Preheat oven to 350 degrees F. Place oven rack in middle of oven. Fit a parchment round cut-to-size into bottom of springform or muffin pan. Spray parchment and sides of springform lightly with cooking spray.

2.
In a medium bowl using a wire whisk beat the whole eggs. Add turbinado sugar, honey, grated pumpkin, pumpkin purée, baking powder, baking soda, ginger, cloves, cinnamon, chia seeds, and flax seeds.

3.
In a separate medium bowl, whisk the almond flour and quinoa flour. Using a silicone spatula gradually fold the flour mixture to the egg mixture to obtain a unified mixture. Add sliced dates to the batter.

4.
Pour into prepared pan. Spread sliced fresh dates and spread slivered almonds over the top of the cake.

5.
Bake in preheated oven approximately 60 minutes until color is light golden brown. Insert toothpick between center and edge comes out clean. Remove from oven and move to rack to cool.

Mazal's Secrets

- **Freeze fresh dates if not ripened**

- **Creating mouthwatering Vegan Bites:** Using a blender, mix 1 ½ cup almonds soaked overnight, 15 fresh dates, 5 medjool dates (without pit, washed), ½ cup mineral water, 2 tablespoons almond butter. Then using a spoon add ¾ cup desiccated coconut (optional) and unify. To achieve a brown color add 2 tablespoons cocoa powder. Form 1" round ball from batter. Roll ball in coconut. Refrigerate or freeze. About 45 servings.

Vegan Bite

Cakes & Almonds

Mazal's Secrets

- Cake is ready when the edges separate from the baking pan.
- Mix dry ingredients and wet ingredients in separate bowls, then add dry ingredients to the wet mixture.
- On Rosh Hashanah substitute almonds for walnuts because in Hebrew the geometric of walnut and sin are the same.

Honey Cake with Pears

~ In our house, sharing pears means sharing love ~

9" round baking pan or 9x5" loaf pan
16 servings
About 250 per serving

Ingredients:
6 large eggs
1 tablespoon freshly squeezed lemon juice
½ cup turbinado sugar
3 soft pears
½ teaspoon baking soda
½ teaspoon baking powder
Grated lemon peel
1 teaspoon cinnamon
¼ teaspoon ginger
¼ teaspoon ground cloves
1 teaspoon molasses (optional)

½ cup strong hot black coffee (add ½ teaspoon instant coffee) OR shot of espresso
¾ cup honey
2 tablespoons of flaxseed
1 teaspoon cocoa powder
1 teaspoon vanilla extract
2 ½ cups blanched almond flour
½ cup gluten-free oatmeal (or quinoa flour)

Streusel Topping:
1 tablespoon turbinado sugar
½ teaspoon cinnamon
⅓ cup of slivered almonds

Method:

1. Preheat oven to 350 degrees F. Place oven rack in middle of oven. Fit a parchment round cut-to-size into bottom of springform pan. Spray parchment and sides of springform lightly with cooking spray.

2. In a mixer, whip egg whites with salt and lemon juice. Add sugar slowly, whip to stiff peaks.

3. In a separate bowl, whisk the egg yolks until slightly foamy. Gently fold in the beaten egg white mixture, making sure the mixture stays well aerated.

4. Slice a pear into 6 or more medium slices and place aside for topping before baking. Use a medium grate for the other 2 pears and add to egg mixture.

5. Prepare hot strong black coffee. Add ½ teaspoon instant coffee, molasses, and honey and stir well using a spoon. Let cool.

6. Whisk the almond flour with the oatmeal flour in a small bowl. Using a silicone spatula gradually fold the flour mixture to the egg mixture. Add coffee mixture and other ingredients to obtain a unified mixture.

7. Pour into prepared pan. Place sliced pear over batter. Sprinkle streusel topping over pear.

8. Bake in preheated oven approximately 30 minutes until light golden brown. Insert toothpick between center and edge comes out clean. Remove from oven and move to rack to cool.

Cakes & Almonds

Apple Cake

~ With tea, coffee or all by itself ~

9" round or square baking pan
16 servings
About 270 per serving

Ingredients:

3 large eggs
1 cup turbinado sugar
Pinch of sea salt
½ cup freshly squeezed lemon juice
½ cup canola oil
1½ cups medium grated apples (red & green apples)
½ cup chopped walnuts
1 cup of raisins
½ teaspoon vanilla extract
2 tablespoon ground flaxseed
2 ¼ cups quinoa flour
½ cup blanched almond flour
1 teaspoon baking soda
1 tablespoon of cinnamon
2 Granny smith apples baked and sliced

Streusel Topping:
½ cup turbinado sugar
½ cup dark brown turbinado sugar
½ teaspoon cinnamon
¼ of slivered almonds
1 medium apple thinly sliced

Mazal's Secrets

- Can replace baked apples with a mixture of apples cooked in 1 cup of water and a ¼ teaspoon of sugar. Strain the liquids.

Method:

1.
Preheat oven to 350 degrees F. Place oven rack in middle of oven. Fit a parchment round cut-to-size into bottom of springform. Spray parchment and sides of springform lightly with cooking spray. Arrange cooked and sliced apples on the bottom.

2.
Using a handheld mixer beat the whole eggs with salt, lemon juice, sugar, and honey.

3.
In a small bowl, whisk quinoa flour and almond flour. Using a silicone spatula gradually fold the flour mixture to the egg mixture.

4.
Add grated apples, oil, walnuts, raisins, vanilla extract, cinnamon, baking powder, baking soda and flax seeds and obtain a unified mixture.

5.
Pour the batter into prepared pan.

6.
Mix the streusel topping: sugar, cinnamon, almonds, and thinly sliced apples and spread over the batter.

7.
Bake in preheated oven approximately 30 to 40 minutes until color is light golden brown. Insert toothpick between center and edge comes out clean. Remove from oven and move to rack to cool.

Cakes & Almonds

Dried and Fresh Fruit Cake
(for Tu B'shvat)

~Who needs food with this duo~

9" round baking pan or 9x5" loaf pan

16 servings
About 210 calories per serving

Ingredients:

3 large eggs
4 tablespoons honey or maple syrup
½ cup agave syrup
2 tablespoon olive oil
2 tablespoon oatmeal
1 teaspoon baking soda
½ teaspoon cinnamon
½ cup of freshly squeezed orange or pomegranate juice
1 fine grated medium orange peel
2½ cups blanched almond flour
¾ cup chopped mixed fresh fruit: pineapple and apples
½ cup chopped nuts (suggestions: hazelnuts, pecans, almonds, and cashews)
½ cup dried fruit (suggestions: raisins, plums, cranberries, fig and dates).

Garnishment:

2 tablespoons mixed chopped nuts
2 tablespoons dried fruit

Method:

1.
Preheat oven to 350 degrees F. Place oven rack in middle of oven. Fit a parchment round cut-to-size into bottom of springform or loaf pan. Spray parchment and sides of springform lightly with cooking spray.

2.
Using a handheld mixer beat the whole eggs with honey, olive oil, agave syrup, baking soda, orange juice, cinnamon and orange peel.

3.
In a small bowl, whisk the almond flour. Using a silicone spatula gradually add the flour mixture to the egg mixture. Add dried fruit, chopped nuts, and fresh fruit and mix to get a unified mixture.

4.
Pour the batter into the prepared pan.

5.
Mix the garnishment: chopped nuts, and dried fruit and spread over the batter.

6.
Bake in preheated oven approximately 25 to 30 minutes until color is light golden brown. Insert toothpick between center and edge comes out clean. Remove from oven and move to rack to cool.

Mazal's Secrets

- Replace the fresh fruit with any seasonal fruit.
- Add 2 tablespoons of flaxseed.

Cakes & Almonds

44 — 45

Mazal's Secrets

- **Play with this cake!** Add a mixture of chia seeds, ½ cup unsweetened desiccated ground coconut, 1 smashed banana, ¼ cup coarsely chopped chocolate.

- Gluten-free all purpose flour can be substituted to rice flour, potato starch, or tapioca flour

- Add 3 tablespoons of chia

Orange Cake

~ Special enough for company ~

Bundt pan or 10" round or square baking pan

16 servings
About 190 calories per serving

Ingredients:

9 large eggs (room temperature)
Pinch of sea salt
2 tablespoons freshly squeezed lemon juice
1 ¼ cup turbinado sugar
1 tablespoon baking powder
2 medium oranges
½ teaspoon vanilla extract
¾ cup quinoa or gluten-free all purpose flour
2 ¼ cups blanched almond flour

Method:

1.
Preheat oven to 350 degrees F. Place oven rack in middle of oven. Spray bundt pan lightly with cooking spray.

2.
In a mixer, whip egg whites with salt, and lemon juice. Add sugar slowly, whip to stiff peaks.

3.
In a separate bowl, whisk the egg yolks until slightly foamy. Gently fold in the beaten egg white mixture, making sure the mixture stays well aerated.

4.
Thoroughly wash oranges and finely grate the peel. Cut the oranges into small pieces, remove the seeds, and blend in mixer. Add grated peel and blended oranges to mixture.

5.
Whisk the almond flour, gluten-free flour, vanilla extract, and baking powder in a medium bowl. Gently fold the flour mixture to the egg mixture using a silicone spatula to obtain a unified mixture.

6.
Pour into prepared pan. Bake in preheated oven approximately 30 minutes until color is light golden brown. Insert toothpick between center and edge comes out clean.

7.
Remove cake from oven and move to rack to cool. Sift powdered sugar on top before serving. Remove from oven and move to rack to cool.

with chia seeds

Cakes & Almonds

Almond Blossom Cake
(Sponge cake)

~ From one recipe, blooms nine different cakes ~

10" round or square baking pan
16 servings
About 190 calories per serving for sponge cake

Sponge Cake (1)
Basic Ingredients:
9 large eggs
A pinch of sea salt
2 tablespoons freshly squeezed lemon juice
2 tablespoons fine lemon zest
1¼ cups turbinado sugar
2¼ cups blanched almond flour
1 teaspoon vanilla extract
1 tablespoon baking powder
½ cup quinoa or gluten-free all purpose flour

For chocolate sponge cake (2)

16 servings 192 calories per serving

add to basic ingredients (1):
3 heaping tablespoons of cocoa powder
(Optional: substitute gluten-free all purpose flour for Teff flour)

For coconut sponge bundt cake (or muffin) (3)

16 servings 220 calories per serving

add to basic ingredients (1):
1 cup of unsweetened ground coconut
Orange zest from medium size orange
(Optional: "for moist coconut sponge cake/muffin" on page 48)

For chocolate chip muffin (4)

16 muffins 210 calories per serving

add to basic ingredients (1):
1 cup of chocolate chips

For fruit sponge cake or muffin (5)

Add to basic ingredients (1): 16 muffins 200 calories per serving
1 cup of sliced fruit (blueberries, apricots, peaches, etc.)

Mazal's Secrets

- The basic sponge cake (1) is fulfilling even without any additions!

- Feel free to use different sizes and shapes of baking or muffin pans.

Almond Blossom
moist coconut cake
(3)

Cakes & Almonds

More Additions and Upgrades for Almond Blossom Cake

~ My lovely granddaughter gave me the inspiration to create healthy doughnuts with this cake batter ~

Method:

1.
Preheat oven to 350 degrees F. Place oven rack in middle of oven. Fit a parchment round cut-to-size into bottom of springform pan. Spray parchment and sides of springform lightly with cooking spray.

2.
In a mixer, whip egg whites with salt, and lemon juice. Add sugar slowly, whip to stiff peaks.

3.
In a separate bowl, whisk the egg yolks until slightly foamy. Gently fold in the beaten egg white mixture, making sure the mixture stays well aerated. Add lemon zest, vanilla extract, and baking powder.

4.
Whisk the almond flour with the gluten-free flour in a medium bowl. Add any remaining ingredients from other cake or muffin recipes (1-9). Using a silicone spatula gradually fold the flour mixture to the egg mixture to obtain a unified mixture.

5.
Pour into prepared pan.

6.
Bake in preheated oven approximately 30 minutes until color is light golden brown (If making muffins, bake for approximately 15-20 minutes). Insert toothpick between center and edge comes out clean. Remove from oven and move to rack to cool.

Honey orange syrup

½ cup freshly squeezed orange juice

2 tablespoons honey (dissolved in a microwave oven)

Add the honey to the orange juice, stir until smooth syrup.

for moist coconut sponge cake/muffin
add 2 tablespoons of orange blossom water or rosewater to the honey orange syrup

for muffin whip cream
add 1 teaspoon of whiskey or brandy extract to the honey orange syrup

Mazal's Secrets

- Quinoa flour is preferred of all other gluten-free flours since it is protein based. It is healthy and good for weight watchers.

- Can substitute equal amounts of dairy products for nondairy.

Cakes & Almonds

Additions and Upgrades
for Basic Cake/Layer Cake

~ Great right out of the fridge! ~

For almond blossom moist coconut sponge bundt cake / muffin (3):

1.
Add 2 tablespoons of the orange blossom water (or rosewater) to the honey orange syrup.

2.
Once the coconut bundt cake or muffin (3) is baked, using a knife separate the cake from the edges of the pan.

3.
Drizzle 2 tablespoons of honey syrup mixed with orange blossom water while the cake is hot.

4.
Flip the cake onto a serving dish. Top with 2 tablespoons sliced blanched almonds and 2 tablespoons ground coconut.

5.
Drizzle the remaining honey syrup mixed with orange blossom water over the cake.
(Double the amount of honey orange syrup for a moister cake.)

For amazing tasting doughnuts (6):

16 servings
About 210 calories per serving

1.
Add to the basic ingredients (1) finely grated orange zest of one large orange

2.
2 tablespoons brandy or 1 teaspoons whiskey extract

3.
Pour batter into any sized muffin pan.

4.
Bake for approximately 15-20 minutes.

5
.Fill with strawberry jam, chocolate spread, or any other spread

6.
Sift powdered sugar on top.

Mazal's Secrets

- Replace instant pudding with 4 tablespoons cornstarch and 2 tablespoons of vanilla sugar.
- When baking it is important to use measuring cups.

Cakes & Almonds

Mazal's Secrets

- Alternate light and dark colors in between layers for the basic layers cake.
- Add fruit between layers.

Additions and Upgrades
for Basic Cake/Layer Cake

For muffin whip cream (Sabrina) (7):

16 servings
About 240 calories per serving

1.
Spray baking oil on muffin or dented silicone cupcake pan and pour the batter of the basic ingredients (1) into prepared pan and bake approximately 20 minutes or until light golden brown. Let it cool.

2.
Thinly slice the muffin top.

3.
Add whiskey/brandy extract to the honey orange syrup and drizzle the mix over the muffin. Optional spread on sliced muffin before decorating with whip cream: natural raspberry jam. Decorate with Rich Whip Liquid non dairy topping (add 1 tablespoon of cocoa to the whip cream for a brown color).

4.
Place back the muffin top on the side.

5.
Decorate with fruit or chocolate. Drizzle honey orange syrup over cupcake again.

For Layer cake (8) (with whipped cream filling):

16 servings
About 240 calories per serving

Ingredients:
1½ cup (12 oz.) Rich Whip Liquid ready to whip cream
4 tablespoons cornstarch + 2 tablespoon vanilla extract (unless using 4 tablespoons vanilla pudding)

Method:

1.
Spray oil on parchment paper and place in loaf baking pan. Pour the batter of the basic ingredients (1) into 2 pans and bake approximately 20 minutes or until golden. Insert toothpick to make sure cake is dry.

2.
Cool the cakes up to a day (or freeze for more even slices) and cut horizontally into two or three slices.

3.
Whip the Rich Whip Liquid whip cream with cornstarch until firm (set aside ½ cup for creamy chocolate below) and spread on each layer.

4.
Decorate the top layer with chocolate cream, whipped cream, cherries, and chocolate curls.

5.
Garnish with fruit.

Decoration: Chocolate cream

½ cup whip cream set aside
1 teaspoon cocoa powder
¼ teaspoon instant coffee
1 tablespoon brandy or rum optional
Mix all ingredients until uniformed cream

8 Layer cake with whipped cream filling

7

Cakes & Almonds

Mazal's Secrets

- Serve the cake as an ice cream sandwich- bake, freeze and cut.

Cold Tofutti Cheesecake
istened with chocolate syrup and tofutti cream cheese filling:

~ A cake rich in protein that is satisfying and delicious! ~

16 servings
About 314 calories per serving

Ingredients:

3 (8oz.) containers Tofutti cream cheese
½ cup (4 oz.) Tofutti sour cream
¾ cup turbinado sugar
1 tablespoon finely grated lemon zest
1 cup (8 oz.) Rich Whip Liquid ready to whip cream
4 tablespoons cornstarch (or just 4 tablespoons vanilla pudding, but exclude vanilla extract)
2 tablespoons of vanilla sugar or vanilla extract
2 tablespoons freshly squeezed lemon juice

Method:

1.
In a hand mixer on high setting mix, Rich Whip cream. Add 4 tablespoons cornstarch and 2 tablespoons of vanilla sugar or vanilla extract (unless using just 4 tablespoons vanilla pudding) until firm.

2.
In a separate bowl, using a hand mixer on low setting, mix Tofutti cream cheese, Tofutti sour cream, lemon juice, lemon zest, and sugar until smooth.

3.
Combine the two mixtures gently using folding motions.

4.
Refrigerate to settle for a few hours.
(Set aside ½ cup for decoration)

Chocolate syrup to spread between cake layers

Ingredients:

1 cup water
¼ cup cocoa powder
3.5 oz.(100g) 60% dark chocolate
½ cup (4 oz.) Tofutti sour cream
1 tablespoon brandy or rum

Chocolate syrup

1.
In a saucepan boil water.

2.
Add cocoa and chocolate and stir until completely dissolved.

3.
Add rum or brandy.

4.
Add Tofutti sour cream

5.
Stir until sauce is smooth.
(put ¼ cup aside for decoration)

Decoration:

The whipped Tofutti cheese topping to decorate the cake:
½ cup of whipped tofutti cream cheese topping with 1/4 cup chocolate syrup.

Cake assembly:

Slice the cake base while cold into three layers (or freeze, then slice for more evenly cut layers).
Optional: (For even layers without slicing), Separate cake batter into 3 same sized pans and bake each separately.

1.
Moisten each slice with chocolate syrup with a tablespoon and spread ⅓ of the cheesecake mixture over it. Place the next layer on top and repeat step for third layer.

2.
Spread the decoration (whipped tofutti cheese topping) around the cake and on top. Using the tip of a fork, decorate the sides of the cake and the top.

3.
Using vegetable peeler, scrape chocolate to create curls for decoration.

For a Delicious Strawberry Shortcake

Ingredients:

Almond Blossom Cake (Basic #1) split in 3 layers
Whipped Cream -16 oz Rich Whipped Cream whipped with 4 tbsp cornstarch and 1 tsp pure vanilla extract
Natural strawberry jam - all fruit
Fresh sliced strawberries

Method:

1.
Spread jam to taste on first layer of cake

2.
spread 1/3 whipped cream and top with sliced strawberries.

3.
Repeat for the other layers.

4.
Decorate with additional strawberries on the top for an amazing finish.

Strawberry Shortcake

Cold Tofutti cheesecake

Cakes & Almonds

Chocolate Marble Cake

~ A cake you'll want to eat every day ~

10" round or square baking pan
16 servings
About 218 calories per serving

Ingredients:

9 large eggs
Pinch of sea salt
1 tablespoon freshly squeezed lemon juice
1¼ cups turbinado sugar
2 cups blanched almond flour
½ cup gluten-free all purpose flour or quinoa flour
1 tablespoon baking powder
3 heaping tablespoons cocoa powder
Optional: ½ medium orange freshly squeezed

Mazal's Secrets

- **To create a marvelous Cinnamon Marble Cake** use the same ingredients as above, but substitute cinnamon for cocoa and add streusel topping: ½ cup sliced almond, 1 tablespoon turbinado sugar, and 1 teaspoon cinnamon on batter before baking.

- Can pour the white mixture in the baking pan, add the brown mixture in the center of the white mixture and marbleize by using a fork in circular motions.

- **Amazing chocolate cake:** mix all ingredients in recipe, just substitute gluten-free all purpose flour for teff flour (for a rich taste, add ¼ cup chopped chocolate to batter).

Method:

1.
Preheat oven to 350 degrees F. Place oven rack in middle of oven. Fit a parchment round cut-to-size into bottom of springform pan. Spray parchment and sides of springform lightly with cooking spray.

2.
In a mixer, whip egg whites with salt and lemon juice. Add sugar slowly, whip to stiff peaks..

3.
In a separate bowl, whisk the egg yolks until slightly foamy. Gently fold in the beaten egg white mixture, making sure the mixture stays well aerated.

4.
Whisk the almond flour with the gluten-free flour in a medium bowl. Using a silicone spatula gradually fold the flour mixture and baking powder to the egg mixture to obtain a unified mixture.

5.
Divide batter into two separate bowls. Add cocoa powder plus orange juice to one of the bowls and fold in gently.

6.
Pour half of white batter in the prepared pan, followed by half of the cocoa batter in the center. Repeat using the remaining batter (make sure to pour batter in center like a target). Using a knife draw back and forth lines to create a pattern.

7.
Bake in preheated oven approximately 30 minutes until color is light golden brown. Insert toothpick between center and edge comes out clean. Remove from oven and move to rack to cool.

marvelous Cinnamon Marble Cake

Cakes & Almonds

Mazal's Secrets

- Cut a length of parchment paper long enough to line the bottom of the pan with extra hanging over the sides to remove loaf bread easier once baked.
- Replace pecans with walnuts.
- Exchange bananas with ⅓ cup tofutti sour cream.

Banana Pecan Bread

This cake is perfect for taking advantage of your ripe bananas and making your home smell fantastic.

9x5" loaf pan
12 servings
About 143 calories per serving

Ingredients:

5 large eggs
Pinch of sea salt
4 teaspoons honey
1 tablespoon tahini paste
¾ cup turbinado sugar (or Truvia)
3 ripe bananas
1 tablespoon vanilla extract
1 tablespoon baking powder
½ teaspoon baking soda
1 cup gluten-free all purpose flour or quinoa flour
1¼ cups fine ground pecans
½ cup chopped pecans

Method:

1.
Preheat oven to 350 degrees F. Place oven rack in middle of oven. Spray loaf pan lightly with cooking spray.

2.
Using a handheld mixer, whip eggs with salt, sugar, honey, and banana. Mix in the tahini paste, vanilla extract, baking soda, baking powder. Mix well to form unified mixture.

3.
In a medium bowl, whisk the flour, ground pecans and chopped pecans. Using a silicone spatula gradually fold in the flour mixture to the egg mixture to obtain a unified mixture. Pour the batter into prepared pan.

4.
Bake for approximately 30 to 40 minutes in the preheated oven until the color is light golden brown. Insert toothpick between center and edge comes out clean.

5.
Remove from oven and move to rack to cool.

Cakes & Almonds

Poppy Snow Cake

~A cake that will make your guests begging for more!~

9" round or square baking pan
16 servings
About 240 calories per serving

Ingredients:

7 large eggs
Pinch of sea salt
¼ cup freshly squeezed lemon juice
1½ cups turbinado sugar
½ medium orange juiced
1 tablespoon orange zest
1 teaspoon grated lemon zest
1 tablespoon instant coffee
2 tablespoons of ground flaxseed
1 tablespoon baking powder
1 cup medium/ground walnuts
1¼ cups blanched almond flour or almond meal
1 cup whole poppy seeds
½ cup of quinoa flour or any gluten-free all purpose flour

Garnish:

Powdered sugar or unsweetened desiccated ground coconut

Method:

1.
Preheat oven to 350 degrees F. Place oven rack in middle of oven. Fit a parchment round cut-to-size into bottom of springform pan. Spray parchment and sides of springform lightly with cooking spray.

2.
In a mixer, whip egg whites with salt and lemon juice. Add sugar slowly, whip to stiff peaks.

3.
In a separate bowl, whisk the egg yolks until slightly foamy. Gently fold in the beaten egg white mixture, making sure the mixture stays well aerated. Put 2 tablespoons of hot water in a cup, add 1 tablespoon of instant coffee, once dissolved, add orange juice and add it to the egg mixture. With a silicone spatula mix in orange zest, lemon zest, flax seeds, baking powder, and walnuts.

4.
Whisk the almond flour with the gluten-free flour in a medium bowl. Gradually fold the flour mixture to the egg mixture. Add poppy seeds and form a unified mixture.

5.
Pour into prepared pan.

6.
Bake in preheated oven approximately 30 minutes until color is light golden brown. Insert toothpick between center and edge comes out clean. Remove from oven and move to rack to cool.

Before serving, sift powdered sugar or coconut on the cake.

Mazal's Secrets

- Egg whites should be at room temperature to achieve stiff peaks.

- Cake is ready when it separates from the baking pan.

- Can add ½ cup unsweetened desiccated ground coconut to cake batter.

Cakes & Almonds

Poppy Seed and Tofu Cheesecake

A cake that not only tastes great, but will bring you compliments even after it's gone!

10" round or square baking pan
16 servings
About 275 calories per serving

1¼ cups whole poppy seeds
1 medium finely grated orange zest
1 teaspoon finely grated lemon zest

Ingredients:

6 large eggs
Pinch of sea salt
½ cup freshly squeezed lemon juice
1 ¼ cup turbinado sugar
1 tablespoon baking powder
8 oz. of Tofutti cream cheese
3 oz of Tofutti sour cream
1½ cups blanched almond flour
½ cup gluten-free oats or quinoa flour

Chocolate coating:

5½ oz. (150 grams) 60% dark chocolate
¼ cup of freshly squeezed orange juice or water
9 oz. Tofutti sour cream cheese
1 tablespoon whiskey extract

Garnishment:

2 oz. of 60% baking chocolate (room temperature)

Mazal's Secrets

- Petit fours pictured :Use only the prepared chocolate topping in this recipe for a delicate chocolate dessert. Just add ½ cup medium chopped hazelnuts to chocolate topping. Pour into petitfours using a spoon. Press hazelnut on top lightly. Store in fridge.
- Can only replace the almond flour with ground nuts, not other flour.
- Tofu can be replaced with dairy, if desired.

Method:

1.
Preheat oven to 350 degrees F. Place oven rack in middle of oven. Fit a parchment round cut-to-size into bottom of springform pan. Spray parchment and sides of springform lightly with cooking spray.

2.
In a mixer, whip egg whites with salt and lemon juice. Add sugar slowly, whip to stiff peaks..

3.
In a separate bowl, using a handheld mixer,on low speed, mix the egg yolks, tofutti cream cheese and a 3 oz. of Tofutti sour cream for a short time just to get it creamy. Using a silicone spatula gently fold in the beaten egg white mixture, making sure the mixture stays well aerated.

4.
Whisk the almond flour with the gluten-free flour in a medium bowl. Using a silicone spatula gradually fold the flour mixture to the egg mixture. Add poppy seeds, baking powder, orange zest, and lemon zest. Mix to form a unified mixture.

5.
Pour into prepared pan.

6.
Bake in preheated oven approximately 50 to 60 minutes until color is light golden brown. Insert toothpick between center and edge comes out clean. Remove from oven and move to rack to cool. Using a knife go around the edges of the pan to make sure it doesn't stick.

7.
Break the chocolate into small pieces. Put chocolate and orange juice in saucepan over medium low heat. Stir occasionally until melted. Take off heat immediately so it won't burn. Then quickly add 9 oz. tofutti sour cream cheese and whiskey extract. Mix to obtain a unified mixture. Using a silicone spatula apply coating over the cooled cake.

8.
For garnishment: Finely grate chocolate and use a vegetable peeler to scrape chocolate curls. Spread over cake. Store in refrigerator.

Cakes & Almonds

Tofu Cheesecake with Berries

~Spoil yourself with a cake that combines color, flavor, and health.~

10" round baking pan
16 servings
About 235 calories per serving

Ingredients:

6 large eggs
Pinch of sea salt
¼ cup freshly squeezed lemon juice
1½ cups turbinado sugar
Zest of a large lemon
4 tablespoons corn starch or vanilla pudding (exclude vanilla extract)
¼ cup blanched almond flour (corn flour or gluten-free all purpose flour)
3 containers (8 oz.) Tofutti cream cheese
1 container (12 oz.) Tofutti sour cream
2 tablespoons vanilla sugar or vanilla extract

Topping
- 3 heaping tablespoons of natural apricot jam
- Berries
- For "tofu cheesecake with chocolate:" on page 68

Mazal's Secrets

- There is no need to preheat the oven, place the baking pan on the bottom shelf. Optional: place disposable aluminum foil pan filled with water on the lowest shelf for a moist cake.

- While the cake is still warm, take a knife and place it between the cake and the pan. Make sure to go around the entire cake to separate it from the pan and prevent it from sticking.

- Tofu can be replaced with dairy, if desired.

Method:

1.
Place oven rack in bottom of cool oven. Fit a parchment round cut-to-size into bottom of springform pan. Spray parchment and sides of springform lightly with cooking spray. Spread ¼ cup almond flour (can use corn starch or gluten-free flour) on the bottom and sides of pan.

2.
Using a handheld mixer, whip egg whites with salt and lemon juice. Add sugar slowly, whip to stiff peaks.

3.
In a separate medium bowl, place the egg yolks, tofutti cheese, tofutti sour cream, lemon zest, cornstarch (or vanilla pudding) and vanilla sugar using low-speed for a short time just to get it creamy. Using a silicone spatula gently fold in the beaten egg white mixture, making sure the mixture stays well aerated.

4.
Pour the batter into prepared pan. Set oven to 350 degrees F. (Don't preheat)

5.
Bake approximately 60 minutes until color is golden brown. Remove from oven, with a knife circle the side of the cake to make sure the cake doesn't stick to the sides of pan and allow it to cool on a rack.

6.
Refrigerate, when cooled, spread apricot jam (if the jam is too thick, soften it by warming it in a microwave oven) and add berries or other fruits desired.

Cakes & Almonds

Topping Options

~It always makes me laugh when my guests discover that my amazing cheesecake is actually made with tofu!~

For tofu cheesecake with chocolate:

On top of the tofu cheesecake, spread apricot jam (microwave if thick) and decorate with 1 cup grated chocolate for baking, ½ cup white chocolate chips, and peel chocolate with a peeler to create chocolate curls.

For fruit cheesecake:

After you make the tofu cheesecake on the bottom of the pan before pouring batter, place chopped fruits such as pineapple or blueberries. When cake cools, spread apricot jam (or any natural jam) on top (microwave if jam is thick) and decorate with the same fruit on top. Decorate with Persimmon in winter (as pictured).

Mazal's Secrets

- *Seasonal fruits, curled chocolates, or chocolate syrup add a rich taste to the cake.*
- *Creating perfect chocolate curls is simple, just peel chocolate at room temperature, not cold.*

{ Soybean is leguminous plant type

Forage developed cultural soybean bar and later developed soybean and tofu only in the 19th century came to Europe and America

Soybean is a source of complete protein - containing all the essential amino acids . In addition , soy is rich B vitamins, iron and minerals such as calcium and magnesium . Soy is used as a substitute for animal protein and protein percentage in Soybean is highest from any vegetable source (it's a great source for vegetarians and vegans)

Tofu (also known as anticoagulation formed by coagulation soymilk)

Tasteless and therefore serves as the basis for countless different recipes

in recent years the tofu western kitchen also recognized as a raw material

Fine with many different specific applications alongside many health benefits .

Health benefits of tofu:

The tofu protein and soy are complete protein . About 95% of the protein is absorbed by the body . Tofu is more rich in calcium compared to cow's milk. It is also low-fat, no cholesterol and is low in calories

No wonder the tofu edible bases diets of billions of people in East Asia for thousands of years and innumerable other dishes and cakes which can be made from it . }

persimmon

Cakes & Almonds

Basic Pie Preparation
(makes two pie crusts)

~This pie has four options for fillings, one of which is filled after baking. Wonderful for the holidays or for a special treat anytime.~

9" pie pan
All pies include basic pie calories

Crust Ingredients:

1 large egg
3 egg yolks
Pinch of sea salt
¼ cup raw tahini paste, coconut, or olive oil
⅔ cup turbinado sugar
1 tablespoon baking powder
½ teaspoon baking soda
1 tablespoon vanilla extract
1 ½ cup gluten-free all purpose flour or quinoa flour
1 ⅓ cup blanched almond flour
Optional: 1 tablespoon orange zest

Method:

1.
In a medium bowl using a fork mix egg, egg yolks, salt, tahini paste, sugar, baking powder, baking soda, and vanilla extract to an airy consistency.

2.
In a medium bowl, whisk the almond flour, gluten free flour, baking powder and baking soda. Using a fork, gradually add the flour mixture into the egg mixture to obtain a unified mixture.

3.
Cover the dough with plastic wrap and refrigerate for one hour. Knead the dough again, if too soft add gluten-free all purpose flour or quinoa flour.

4.
Roll out half of the amount of the basic pie on a floured (gluten-free) work surface. (Store the other half in freezer or use it to make another pie.) Firmly press half of the dough into bottom and sides of oiled pie pan. Use one of the options for pie filling on the next page (poppy seed, mixed nut, or pumpkin filling).

5.
Bake in preheated oven approximately 30 minutes until color is light golden brown.

Please note: for cold cheese fillings, first bake the dough without the filling (covered with parchment paper for 10 minutes). Then remove the paper and bake again until light golden brown.

Mazal's Secrets

- Can bake the pie crust in a square pan and after baking, spread jam, chocolate cream, fill and decorate with nuts... feel free to use your imagination!

- Use a removable-bottom pie pan – it is easier to remove when the pie is ready.

- Mini pie cheese cream filling see, "Cold Tofutti cheesecake" on page 54 or use whipped cream or yogurt and garnish with fruits, nuts or cookie crumbs.

- Prepare dough and freeze to use later.

Mixed Nut Pie

Mini pie

Cakes & Almonds

Mazal's Secrets

- **For Pecan Pie,** substitute 1 cup of chopped pecans for the hazelnuts, and walnuts. Garnish with pecan halves tossed with 2 tablespoons Turbinado sugar and ¼ teaspoon cinnamon.

- Bake remainder of basic pie dough recipe in a separate pan and crumble for a fun garnish.

- Raisins can be added to the poppy seed mixture.

Basic Pie Fillings

~Leaves a craving for more!~

For Poppy Seed Pie

16 servings
About 275 calories per serving

Ingredients:
½ basic pie dough recipe

Making the filling:
1 large egg
Pinch of sea salt
1 tablespoon freshly squeezed lemon juice
1½ cups almond milk (water or freshly squeezed orange juice)
1½ cups turbinado sugar
1 tablespoon whiskey or brandy
1 apple, medium grated
¼ cup blanched almond flour or almond meal
2 tablespoons gluten-free all purpose flour
10.5 oz. (300g) whole poppy seeds
2 tablespoon dried cranberries
½ cup unsweetened desiccated ground coconut (optional)
(Optional: above filling can be substituted with 12.5 oz (1 can) poppy seed filling. Add cranberries, whisky, all the flour and optional coconut.)

Method:
1. Preheat oven to 350 degrees F. Place rack in the middle of oven. Spray baking spray lightly on pan and press ½ basic dough into pan and along sides.
2. **Start making the filling:** In a medium saucepan, bring almond milk (or other choice of liquid) to boil. Add sugar and poppy seeds while mixing with spoon. Cook for about 5 minutes using low heat.
3. Take off the heat and add lemon, apple and cranberries. Add whiskey or brandy, blanched almond flour and gluten-free flour.
4. Cool the batter.
5. In a small bowl, whisk the egg and add it to cooled batter and mix rapidly upon adding.
6. Pour filling or optional ready filling into prepared pan. Bake for approximately 30 minutes until crust is golden.

Mixed Nut Pie (almond, walnuts, hazelnuts)

16 servings
About 200 calories per serving

Ingredients:
½ basic pie dough recipe

Making the filling:
1 large eggs
Pinch of sea salt
1 tablespoon freshly squeezed lemon juice
½ cup turbinado sugar
1 tablespoon whiskey or brandy
12 oz. Tofutti sour cream
½ tablespoon cinnamon
2 tablespoons cocoa powder
½ cup medium raw ground hazelnut
½ cup medium raw ground walnut
½ cup blanched almond flour or almond meal

Streusel Topping:
¼ cup of mixed coarsely chopped raw hazelnut and almond

Method:
1. Preheat oven to 350 degrees F. Place oven rack in middle of oven. Spray pie pan lightly with baking spray and firmly press dough from ½ basic pie dough into bottom and sides.
2. In a small bowl using a wire whisk, mix egg whites, salt, sugar and lemon. In a separate bowl whip the egg yolks, whiskey, sour cream, cinnamon, and cocoa powder. Fold the egg yolk into the egg white mixture.
3. Using a silicone spatula gradually add ground hazelnut, ground walnut and almond flour to the egg mixture.
4. Pour batter into prepared pie pan. Top the batter with coarsely chopped hazelnut and walnut.
5. Bake for approximately 30 minutes until crust is golden.

Cakes & Almonds

Mazal's Secrets

- You can skip some types of nuts and use whatever is available in the pantry.

- **For delicious Apple Pie,** substitute pumpkin with 1 cup grated apples and 1 cup sliced apples. Garnish with sliced apples, 2 tablespoons Turbinado sugar and ¼ teaspoon cinnamon, combined. Save ¼ of basic pie dough for topping: Roll dough into long pieces and place on top to achieve lattice top.

- Use banana squash mixed with sweet potato instead of pumpkin.

- Rather than using spices in ingredients, mixed pie spices are sold readily!

Pumpkin Pie Cheesecake

~My client Sari doesn't like pumpkin but loves this pumpkin pie cheesecake and asked for the recipe!~

9" Pie baking pan
16 servings
About 125 calories per serving

Ingredients:

½ the amount of basic pie dough recipe
2 cups fresh pumpkin pulp (or canned, without preservatives)
2 large eggs, lightly beaten
Pinch of sea salt
1 teaspoon freshly squeezed lemon juice
1 ¼ cup turbinado sugar
8 oz. container Tofutti cream cheese (227 grams)
12 oz. Tofutti sour cream
½ cup blanched almond flour or almond meal
1 tablespoon cinnamon
1 teaspoon ginger
¼ teaspoon ground nutmeg
¼ teaspoon ground cloves
¼ teaspoon cardamom powder

Garnish:
2 tablespoons turbinado sugar
¼ cup sliced almonds
¼ teaspoon ground cinnamon (optional)

Method:

1.
Preheat oven to 350 degrees F. Place oven rack in middle of oven. Spray pie pan lightly with baking spray and firmly press dough from ½ basic pie dough into bottom and sides.

2.
In a small bowl using a wire whisk, mix egg, salt, sugar and lemon.

3.
In a pot filled with water cook pumpkin until soft and fork goes through. Blend in a food processor on low speed. Keep only 2 cups of blended pumpkin pulp in processor. Add cream cheese, and sour cream. Add the egg mixture and the remaining ingredients mix until unified mixture achieved.

4.
Pour filling into prepared pie pan. Garnish over the batter with turbinado sugar, sliced almonds and ground cinnamon.

5.
Bake for approximately 30 minutes until crust is golden. Remove from oven and move to rack to cool.

❝ **Cookies:** Filling and can be exchanged for a meal! The best recipes for cookies are made with all natural and organic ingredients:

Almonds, walnuts, a variety of seeds, gluten-free oatmeal, dried and fresh fruits, raw sesame butter, almond butter, peanut butter, olive oil, gluten-free flours, pure honey, and sugar cane.

These ingredients are not only satisfying and tasty, but they serve to regulate the colon and help prevent eating disorders. The cookies, like the rest of the pastries in the book, are rich in protein and free of gluten, trans fatty oils, white flour, and milk. In order to maintain a stable weight, it's recommended to lower the consumption of corn flour, peanuts, and sunflower seeds which are high in fat and trick the body into thinking it's hungry. Better ingredient choices are: raw almonds, raw walnuts or raw pumpkin seeds.

Flour: The almond flour cannot be substituted for any recipes (hence the name of the book!), but all the gluten-free flour (except almond flour) in the recipes can be changed to other types of flour. I recommend flours such as quinoa, tapioca, soy, oatmeal, dura, white rice, brown rice, potato, teff, and mixed gluten-free flours. Teff flour alters the color and texture of recipes, but it's still amazing. I recommend using it for the darker colored cookies and cakes. The beauty of using almond flour or other raw nuts is that they don't lose their nutritional value in the baking process.

I have created my personal mix of gluten-free flours by mixing equal amounts of white and brown rice, potato flour and tapioca. ❞

Cookies

COOKIES

Tahini Cookies
(Sesames, Dates and Poppy Seed)

~ A cake rich in protein that is satisfying and delicious! ~

36 cookies
Cookie sheets
Serving size 2 cookies
About 142 calories

Ingredients:

2 large eggs
A pinch of sea salt
4 tablespoons honey
¼ cup turbinado sugar
2 tablespoons tahini paste
½ teaspoon vanilla extract
2½ cups blanched almond flour
½ teaspoon baking powder or baking soda

Filling:

- Use whole poppy seed filling hamantaschen ("Poppy Seed filling" on page 74), pre-made canned poppy seed filling, jam or chocolate filling.
- ½ medjool date without the stem and ½ a raw walnut

-check dried fruit for worms-

Topping:

Sesame seeds (for tahini cookie). OR Powdered sugar (for date cookies)

Method:

1.
Beat eggs with salt, honey, agave, tahini and vanilla extract.

2.
Whisk the blanched almond flour and baking powder and using a fork gradually fold it into the egg mixture to obtain a unified mixture.

3.
Cover with parchment paper and fridge for one hour. (If dough is too soft add more almond flour)

4.
Set oven to 350 degrees F. Line two baking sheets with parchment paper. Spray parchment paper with cooking spray lightly.

5.
Drop tablespoons of dough onto prepared pan 2" apart. Using your hands flatten the dough. Refer to preparation below for remaining ingredients for tahini sesame cookies, poppy seed triangle, or date cookies.

6.
Bake in preheated oven approximately 12 to 15 minutes or until lightly brown. Remove from oven and move to rack to cool.

Preparation:

For tahini sesame cookie:
Sprinkle sesame seeds
Optional: For chocolate chip cookies, mix ½ cup chocolate chips in dough.

For poppy seed triangle (Hamantashen):
Place 1 teaspoon poppy seed spread (optional: apricot, raspberry jam or chocolate spread) in the center of each disc. Using your hands fold in the sides of the disc towards the center forming a triangle.

For date cookies:
Place half a date with a walnut in the center of the cookie or "For date filling" on page 84).
Press it into the cookie dough and fold the edges of the dough to cover the filling.

- Pinch the top with pincer puller tweezer or fork
- Bake for 7-12 minutes until golden brown
- Cool and before serving sift powdered sugar on top

Mazal's Secrets

- Use several fillings in the same batch of cookies by dividing dough.
- Mixing ground nuts, cinnamon and maple syrup combined make a great filling.

Manna Cookies
(basic cookie dough)

~ My client, Sandy, says these crispy cookies are like manna from heaven! ~

Cookies:	(4), (5), (9)	(1), (2) (3), (6), (10), (11)	(8)	(7)
Serving size:	2 cookies	2 cookies	2 cookies	2 cookies
Calories:	115	195	230	215

Ingredients (for basic dough):

1 large egg
3 egg yolks
Pinch of sea salt
¼ cup raw tahini paste, olive oil, or coconut oil
⅔ cup turbinado sugar or powdered sugar
1 tablespoon baking powder
½ teaspoon baking soda
1 tablespoon vanilla extract
1 ½ cup gluten-free all-purpose flour or quinoa flour,
1 1/3 cup blanched almond flour
1 tablespoon orange zest (optional)
Extra gluten-free all purpose flour for forming cookies

Method:

1.
In a medium bowl using a fork mix egg, egg yolks, salt, tahini paste, sugar, baking powder, baking soda, orange zest, and vanilla extract to an airy consistency.

2.
With a fork, whisk the almond flour, and quinoa flour gradually into the egg mixture to obtain a unified mixture.

3.
Cover the dough with plastic wrap and refrigerate for one hour. Knead the dough again, if too soft add gluten-free all purpose flour or quinoa flour.

4.
Preheat oven to 350 degrees F. Place oven rack in middle of oven. Line two baking sheets with parchment paper. Spray parchment lightly with cooking spray.

5.
On a floured (gluten-free) work surface roll the dough out to create a roll. If the dough is too soft add some flour. Make 36 even slices (depending on cookie size desired). Using hands flatten each disc.

6.
Fill using options from next page such as Nut, Date, or Poppy Seed filling.

7.
Bake in preheated oven approximately 10-12 minutes or until golden brown

8.
Take cookies out of oven and let cool on rack.
Store in tight container
About 30-36 cookies

COOKIES

Mazal's Secrets

- For Anise cookies, substitute 1 tablespoon anise for the orange zest.
- For flakier cookies use tahini paste or olive oil

9

1

4

7 6 10

COOKIES

Manna Basic Cookies (filling)

Options for fillings

For date filling: (1)

18 pitted Medjool dates
½ cup chopped nuts (walnuts and almonds)
¼ teaspoon cinnamon
7 teaspoons hot water

With a fork, mash the dates with hot water. Add chopped nuts and mix to form a thick mixture. (Alternately, use a half date and half walnut pressed inside cookie dough. Easy and excellent!)

For mixed nut filling: (2)

1½ cups medium ground walnuts
3 tablespoons agave syrup or honey
1 tablespoon cinnamon

For whole poppy seed filling: (3)

Method:

1.
Form basic cookie dough into approximately 36 or more balls, then flatten each ball with the palm of hand.

2.
Place 1 teaspoon poppy seed spread (optional: apricot, raspberry jam or chocolate spread) in the center of each disc. Using your hands fold in the sides of the disc towards the center forming a triangle. ("For Poppy Seed filling" on page 74).

3.
Place cookies 2" apart on the two prepared pans. Bake approximately 10-12 minutes until light golden brown. Remove from oven and allow to completely cool on rack.

We fill and create cookies of various shapes

Almond cookies: (4)

Basic cookie dough
1. Add to dough ¼ teaspoon vanilla extract.
2. Create ball(s) push an almond into the center of each before baking.
refer to secret for filling

Vanilla round bagels: (5)

1 basic cookie dough
1 egg yolk
¼ cup vanilla sugar

Create balls.
Roll each ball to form a cylinder and attach end to a circle.
Brush with egg yolk and sprinkle with vanilla sugar.

Stuffed sticks: (6)

Roll basic cookie dough to equal balls.
Using hands, flatten each ball to form a disc.
Fill each disc with mixed nut filling or date filling close to form a ball and roll to form a stick.

For Biscotti: (7)

1.
Use the basic cookie dough prepared in method above.

2.
Add 1 teaspoon (or more to taste) Anise seed extract, sesame seeds, or ground anise seeds to dough.

3.
Add 1 cup mixture of chopped or sliced almonds, ¾ cup raisins or dried cranberries
(Optional: for chocolate chips cookies omit anise).

4.
Form 2 long flat loaves on the two prepared pans.

5.
For streusel topping mix 1 tablespoon turbinado sugar and 1 teaspoon cinnamon and sprinkle over the loaves.

6.
Bake for approximately 15-20 minutes until golden brown.

7.
Take out of oven and place on a rack to cool. Once cool, slice the loaves in biscotti shape.

8.
Bake again for approximately 10 minutes and leave in oven to cool for extra crispy biscottis.

Mazal's Secrets

- For almond cookies (4), fill with marzipan (see "Marzipan" on page 106)

- This dough makes great biscotti. For chocolate biscotti, substitute Teff flour for gluten-free all purpose flour, add 1 tablespoon cocoa powder and ½ cup chocolate chips.

- For crispy cookies, allow cookies to sit in oven but for moist cookies move cookies with parchment paper slowly onto a rack to cool.

Basic Manna Cookies
(Variations)

~ A cake rich in protein that is satisfying and delicious! ~

For Pecan balls: (8)

1.
Use the basic cookie dough prepared and add ½ cup chopped pecans, 2 teaspoons turbinado sugar, ½ teaspoon cinnamon, and ½ cup raisins, chopped prunes or dates to dough. Using hands form a unified mixture.

2.
Roll 36 even balls from dough (can roll balls in chopped pecans).

3.
Bake for approximately 15-20 minutes until golden brown.

Half a moon cookies: (9)

Basic cookie dough

1.
Roll into balls then shape dough into moon shape

2.
Sift powdered sugar once cookie cools

Date filled cookies: (1)

Basic cookie dough

1.
Place either ½ teaspoon from date filling (page before) or half a date with a walnut in the center of the cookie.

2.
Press it into the cookie dough fold the edges of the dough to cover the filling.

3.
Pinch the top with pincer puller tweezer or fork

4.
Bake no more than 10-12 minutes

5.
Remove parchment with cookies on it to cooking rack. Or, leave on cookie sheet while cooling for softer cookies.

6.
Cool and sift powdered sugar before serving

2 Rolls filled with dates and mixed nuts: (2)

Basic cookie dough

Roll dough

Divide into 2

Flatten and place either date filling or mixed nut filling ("For date filling" on page 84)

Fold edges and then roll

Brush egg yolk

Spread a mix of turbinado sugar and cinnamon

Bake until golden

Cool and Cut (sift powdered sugar before serving-optional)

Swirl shaped cookies: (10)

Follow ingredients for (2)

Place any desired filling and

Before baking, Cut and place each on its side (to achieve swirl shape) and bake until golden

Date filled and sesame topped cookies: (11)

Basic cookie dough

Divide into balls

Fill with half medjool date or date filling

- Press and flatten each cookie
- Create moon or round shape (press fork into edges to get design.)
- Brush with egg yolk (if adding sesame topping)
- Press the edges with fork (for moon shaped)

Mazal's Secrets

- Create a variety of cookies at once by dividing the basic manna dough to use with different fillings.

- Roll the biscuit recipe (7) into a long loaf, freeze it, then cut the frozen loaf into thin slices, and place it on wax paper that is sprayed with baking oil and place it right away into the preheated 350 degree oven until golden.

- To make moroccan biscuits instead of biscotti: spread batter evenly in tray, and spread 1/4 cup mix sesame seeds and anis seeds on top

- The biscotti batter can also be thinly sliced before baking.

COOKIES

COOKIES

Pumpkin Seed Cookies

~ A cake rich in protein that is satisfying and delicious! ~

16" x 22" oven tray
36 cookies (depending on size)
Serving size 2 cookies
About 166 calories

Ingredients:

2 medium eggs
8 tablespoons canola oil
1 cup blanched almond flour or almond meal
2 tablespoons rice flour
1 tablespoon ground flax seed
1 tablespoon chia seeds
9 tablespoons turbinado sugar
1 teaspoon baking powder
½ teaspoon baking soda
3 tablespoons golden raisins
3 cups pumpkin seeds

Method:

1.
Preheat oven to 350 degrees F. Line two baking sheets with parchment paper. Spray parchment paper with cooking spray lightly.

2.
Whisk eggs, sugar, oil, almond flour, rice flour, flax seeds, chia seeds, baking powder, baking soda, raisins, and pumpkin seeds to form a unified mixture.

3.
Drop tablespoons of dough onto prepared pan 2" apart.

4.
Bake in preheated oven approximately 18 to 20 minutes or until lightly brown and firm to touch.

5.
Let it completely cool before separating Store in tight container

Mazal's Secrets

- Easier alternative to using tablespoon: flatten the batter on baking paper, bake 10 mins, cut into square or rectangle shape, and continue to bake until golden brown.

- Leave the baked cookies in the oven while the oven door is open. It is easy to separate the cookies when cool.

- Keep cookies more fresh by storing in the freezer.

Sesame Tahini Cookies

Finishes faster than light can travel

Two 16" x 22" oven tray
36 cookies (depending on size)
About 170 calories (2 cookies)

Ingredients:

2 large eggs
8 tablespoons turbinado sugar
6 tablespoon canola oil or olive oil
4 tablespoons tahini paste
1 tablespoon baking powder
½ teaspoon baking soda
3 cups sesame seed
2 tablespoons rice flour or corn starch

Method:

1.
Preheat oven to 350 degrees and line oven tray with parchment paper. Spray baking spray lightly.

2.
In a medium bowl, using whisk eggs, sugar, tahini paste, oil, baking powder, baking soda, rice flour or cornstarch and sesame seed to form a unified mixture.

3.
Flatten the dough on the baking paper evenly.

4.
Bake for approximately 10 minutes or until firm.

5.
Mark elongated squares on the dough. Cut using a knife on the marked lines and continue to bake until golden brown.

6.
Let cool in the open oven (it is easier to separate the cookies while cold).

Mazal's Secrets

- Can use 8 tablespoons of canola oil instead of tahini paste to get different and more light texture
- Can put ½ cup sunflower or pumpkin seeds

Peanut Butter Oat Cookies

~I keep this on the counter as a favorite for my grandchildren~

Two 16" x 22" oven tray
45 cookies (depending on size)
About 225 calories (2 cookies)

Ingredients:

2 large eggs
2 tablespoons olive oil (coconut, or canola oil)
1 teaspoon vanilla extract
Pinch of sea salt
1 cup dark brown turbinado sugar
½ cup turbinado sugar
1 teaspoon baking soda
½ teaspoon cinnamon
1 cup chunky peanut butter (or almond butter)
3 cups gluten-free oats
¾ cup white chocolate chips
½ cup dried cranberries
1 cup coarsely chopped walnuts or (a mixture of pumpkin seed, pecan, cashew nut or almonds)

Method:

1.
Preheat oven to 350 degrees and line two baking sheets with parchment paper. Spray parchment paper with baking spray lightly.

2.
In a medium bowl, beat eggs with oil, sugar, salt, peanut butter, vanilla, baking soda, cinnamon. Add oats, chocolate chips, cranberries, and walnuts and form a unified mixture.

3.
Drop tablespoons of dough onto baking sheets 2" apart. Form round cookies using two teaspoons.

4.
Bake in preheated oven for approximately 12 to 15 minutes or until lightly brown and firm to touch. Remove from oven and move to rack to cool.

Mazal's Secrets

(P) *For Passover option, use equal amount of crushed gluten free matzo (matzah) instead of oatmeal...absolutely amazing!*

PEANUT BUTTER COOKIES: *mix 1 large egg, ⅓ cup honey, and 1 cup peanut butter, and ½ cup chocolate chips (white or brown), fridge for about an hour, spread parchment paper, spray baking spray lightly, drop tablespoons of dough onto prepared parchment paper. Press fork down on cookie for design. Bake for 7 minutes and enjoy!*

Store cookies only when completely cool.

{ Oats }

Oats special health properties enabling it to absorb gastrointestinal sugar and cholesterol and remove them from the body. Oats creates a feeling of satiety, rich in protein, calcium and vitamin B is important for metabolism.

This is one of the richest foods on the menu, are beneficial to health, overflowing Soluble dietary fiber highest level of cereal family.

These health properties help keep the heart healthy, blood vessels, Digestive system helps in reducing weight, energy and satisfaction Recommended People with problems of sugar, cholesterol and celiac patients **(only when Excellent for gluten-free packaging)**

COOKIES

94 — 95

Mazal's Secrets

(P) *Passover option, use equal amount of crushed gluten-free matzo (matzah) instead of oatmeal...absolutely amazing!*

- *Use a mixture of dried fruit: cranberries, chopped apricots, plums and more.*
- *Look for gluten-free oats at health food stores.*
- *Cookies made of ingredients without preservatives can spoil quickly and should be*
- *Kept in the refrigerator or freezer.*

Granola-Sesame Cookies

16" x 22" oven tray
32 servings (depending on size)
About 172 calories per serving

Ingredients:

3 large eggs
Pinch of sea salt
¾ cup dark brown turbinado sugar
7 tablespoons canola or coconut oil
3 tablespoons agave syrup
½ cup honey
1 teaspoon molasses (optional)
2 tablespoons tahini paste or almond butter
1/3 cup chopped almonds
1 cup sesame seeds
2 tablespoons chia seeds
2 tablespoons ground flax seeds
½ cup pumpkin seeds
½ cup raisins or dried fruit (see secret)
1 teaspoon baking soda or 1 tablespoon baking powder
3 cups gluten-free oats
2 chopped medjool dates

Method:

1.
Preheat oven to 350 degrees and line oven tray with parchment paper. Spray baking spray lightly.

2.
In a medium bowl, using a wire whisk eggs, sugar, oil, molasses, honey, agave tahini paste and baking soda.

3.
Add almonds, sesame seeds, chia seeds, flax seeds, pumpkin seeds, dried fruit, and gluten free oats, dates and form a unified mixture.

4.
Flatten dough using a silicone spatula evenly on the cookie sheet and mark squares using a knife.

5.
Bake approximately 10 minutes. Mark elongated squares on the dough. Cut using a knife on the marked lines and continue to bake approximately 10-15 minutes until golden brown. Remove from oven and move to rack to cool.

COOKIES

Oatmeal-Chia Cookies

16" x 22" oven tray
45 cookies (depending on size)
About 225 calories (2 cookies)

Ingredients:

2 large eggs
Pinch of sea salt
½ cup canola (coconut or olive) oil
4 tablespoons tahini paste
½ cup dark brown turbinado sugar
1 cup turbinado sugar
½ cup applesauce
1 teaspoon vanilla extract
1½ cup quinoa flour
½ cup chia seed
1 tablespoon baking soda
¼ teaspoon cinnamon
3 cups gluten-free oats
¾ cup raisins
1 cup chopped nuts (walnuts and almonds mixed)
½ cup chocolate chips

Method:

1.
Preheat oven to 350 degrees and line two baking sheets with parchment paper. Spray parchment paper with baking spray lightly.

2.
Beat eggs with salt, oil, sugar, applesauce, tahini, vanilla, quinoa flour, chia seeds, baking soda, cinnamon, oats, raisins, chopped nuts, chocolate chips, and form a unified mixture.

3.
Drop tablespoons of dough mixture onto prepared parchment paper 2" apart. Form round cookies.

4.
Bake in preheated oven for approximately 15-20 minutes or until lightly brown. Remove from oven and move to rack to cool. Store in container.

Mazal's Secrets

(P) *For Passover option, use equal amount of crushed gluten-free matzo (matzah) instead of oatmeal...absolutely amazing!*

Save any pieces remaining to use as granola

Easy bake: flatten dough on baking paper. Bake for 10 minutes, remove from oven and using a knife go back and forth to form square cookie marks, continue to bake for approximately 10 minutes until lightly browned. Slice using a knife on the marked lines. Let it cool before separating.

COOKIES

Biscotti

On a chilly day, treat yourself with herbal tea and biscotti

16" x 22" oven tray
32 cookies
About 240 calories (2 cookies)

Ingredients:

6 large egg whites
3 egg yolks
Pinch of sea salt
¼ cup freshly squeezed lemon juice
1¼ cup turbinado sugar
1 tablespoon fine orange zest
3 cups blanched almond flour
⅓ cup quinoa flour or any other gluten-free all-purpose flour
1 teaspoon vanilla extract
1 teaspoon almond extract
1 tablespoon baking powder
1 ½ cup sliced raw almonds
½ cup raisins or dried cranberries

Method:

1.
Preheat oven to 350 degrees F and line oven tray with parchment paper. Spray baking spray lightly.

2.
In a mixer, whip egg whites with salt, lemon juice and sugar until slightly foamy then add the egg yolks.

3.
By hand, using a silicone spatula, add fine orange zest, vanilla extract, almond extract,1 cup sliced almonds, raisins or cranberries and mix well.

4.
In a medium bowl, using a wire whisk, mix the almond flour, quinoa flour, and baking powder.

5.
Using a silicone spatula gradually fold the flour mixture into the the egg mixture to obtain a unified mixture.

6.
Pour the batter (batter should appear cake-like) onto prepared parchment paper and sprinkle ½ cup almond and dried fruit on top.

7.
Bake approximately 20-30 minutes. Remove the tray from oven. Using a knife create horizontal lines and vertical lines to achieve Biscotti style.

8.
Lower the oven heat to 320 degrees F and continue to bake for approximately 20 minutes or more until cookies are dry. Turn off the oven and allow it to cool in the oven. Allow it to completely cool before separating. If the cookies are not crispy, bake again for 3 to 5 minutes.

Mazal's Secrets

- Cool cookies in the open oven (it is easier to separate cookies when completely cold).

Almond Cookies

16" x 22" oven tray
28 cookies (depending on size)
About 227 calories (2 cookies)

Ingredients:

2 egg whites
1 tablespoon freshly squeezed lemon
Pinch of sea salt
¾ cup turbinado sugar
1 teaspoon vanilla extract
4 cups sliced raw almonds or coarsely chopped hazelnuts (see secret for pictured mixed nut cookie)

Method:

1.
Preheat oven to 350 degrees F and line oven tray with parchment paper. Spray baking spray lightly.
2.
In a small bowl, beat egg whites, lemon, salt, and vanilla.
3.
Add sliced almonds or hazelnuts to egg mixture. With a silicone spatula form a unified mixture.
4.
Drop tablespoons of mixture onto prepared parchment paper 2" apart.
5.
Bake in preheated oven for approximately 17 minutes until golden brown.
6.
Remove from oven. Place tray on rack and allow it to cool completely before separating.
Store in tight container

Mazal's Secrets

- *Replace almonds with pecans (delicious!).*

- **Mixed nut cookie:** *substitute 4 cups of raw sliced almonds, sesame seeds, pumpkin seeds in the ingredients with 2 cups almond, 1 cup sesame, 1 cup pumpkin seed, ½ cup raisins make wonderful cookies.*

Weight Issues:

Many people think of cakes, treats, or baked goods as something that is either just for dessert or fattening....or both! The recipes in this book will introduce you to wholesome, healthy ingredients that actually make cake GOOD for you! As with all good things, moderation is the key and one should key an eye on their portions – no matter how good it tastes!

In making healthy choices for your life, it is important to refrain from processed and artificial ingredients that are addicting and create cravings for sweets. They interfere with your metabolism and thus make it hard to lose weight. Beware of: margarine, all sweet juices, food coloring, corn syrup (which exists in all processed cookies and snacks), and preservatives. Also, the Number One ingredient that is the most addictive and harmful of them all: sugar substitute!

Unique Treats

Unique Treats

Vegan Energy Bars (No-bake)

This treat can be frozen, but it is too good to resist once you know you have it!

24 servings
About 204 calories per serving

Ingredients:

12 Medjool dates
10 plums
½ cup raisins
¼ cup halved raw pecans
¼ cup halved raw walnuts
¼ cup raw whole cashew nuts
¼ cup raw whole hazelnuts
¾ cup raw whole almonds
1 tablespoon maple syrup
1 tablespoon ground flax seeds
1 tablespoon chia seeds
2 heaping tablespoons chunky peanut butter (can use tahini paste or almond butter)

Streusel topping:

½ cup unsweetened desiccated ground coconut or medium chopped walnuts

Method:

1.
Take the stem out of the medjool dates, and check all the dried fruit for worms.

2.
Once clean, finely chop dates, plums and raisins on a chopping board.

3.
Place dried fruit in a small bowl and add peanut butter, maple syrup, pecans, walnuts, cashews, hazelnuts, almonds, flax and chia seeds.

4.
Knead wearing gloves or with wet hands to form a unified mixture. Place mixture on parchment paper and use paper to form a cylinder around mixture. Roll it until it looks cylindrical. Freeze for 3 or more hours.

5.
Optional: before serving slice into two even parts. Roll one part in coconut and the second in chopped walnuts.

6.
Slice and serve.
Store in freezer

Mazal's Secrets

- Add ½ a cup of rice crispy to the ingredients.

- Form mixture into balls and roll each in either unsweetened/desiccated ground coconut or rice crispy.

Unique Treats

Marzipan

I recommend this treat for when you have surprise guests, since it is ready to serve out of the freezer!

36 servings
About 40 calories per serving

Ingredients:

2 cups of blanched almond flour
¾ cup turbinado sugar
⅓ cup mineral water
1½ teaspoons freshly squeezed lemon juice
1½ teaspoons almond extract

Garnishment:

36 whole blanched almonds
Melted chocolate or chocolate tahini (recipe on the next page)

Method:

1.
In a medium skillet boil water, sugar, and lemon turn to low heat immediately after boil.

2.
Keep on low heat approximately 10-20 minutes until it becomes sticky.

3.
Add almond extract and turn off the heat. Using a spoon, mix the blanched almond flour and form a unified mixture.

4.
Cover the dough with plastic wrap and refrigerate for about an hour until firm.

5.
Knead and roll, the mixture to form a ball. Form small balls, with your thumb press down the center. Insert an almond in the center of each ball. For a variety, dip one side of ball in melted chocolate. Place in either a tray or decorated cupcake sleeve.

6.
Store in freezer.

Time to play with Marzipan!

Marzipan chocolate filling
28 servings
About 65 calories per serving

Marzipan filling: In any mould soft silicone tray, form the previously prepared or frozen marzipan into any shape that will fit the tray and press with a finger press the middle down, place a hazelnut inside and pour the warm chocolate tahini treat over it. (refer to recipe on next page) Allow it to cool and store in freezer. Serve frozen. Optional: after freezing decorate with hazelnut on top.

Mazal's Secrets

- Recommended lightly wet fingers to prevent sticking.
- Insert a dried cherry in the middle.
- Perfect frozen and can be used as decoration for any occasion to form any shape (flowers, hearts, numbers, etc.)

Unique Treats

Chocolate Tahini Sweets

~In lieu of giving your children and grandchildren candies full of unhealthy preservatives, give your loved ones nutritious chocolate tahini sweets filled with love.~

24 servings
About 64 calories per serving (rectangular sweets)

Ingredients:

8.5 oz. (250g) 60% dark chocolate
1 cup of 100% raw tahini paste
1 cup coarsely chopped raw almond (or brown rice crisps)

Streusel topping:

½ cup coarsely chopped almond, unsweetened desiccated ground coconut or brown rice crisps

Method:

1.
In a medium skillet melt the chocolate on low heat and gradually add tahini paste. Mix until smooth. Remove from heat.

2.
Add 1 cup of almonds (or brown rice crisps) and mix to a smooth chocolate cream.

3.
Pour the batter into a small 12"x6" pyrex or silicone tray (depending on how thick you want the sweets). Garnish with either almond or coconut. For a variety, while the chocolate is hot, top each half with a different streusel topping. Garnish half with coconut and other half with chopped almonds as pictured.

4.
Let it to cool and store in freezer. After frozen, remove it from the tray onto a cutting board. Using a large knife, cut into small rectangles (or any shape) before serving.
Store in freezer.

Play with different fillings for your sweet (refer to secrets)

28 servings
About 65 calories per serving (stuffed petit fours)

Brown and white marzipan fill:

To create petifores (brown and white colors) blend the chocolate and tahini while hot and pour into mould soft silicone tray half way, add previously prepared marzipan ball (check marzipan recipe) in the middle of each serving. Store in freezer. (refer to secret for a peanut butter filling that children love).

Mazal's Secrets

- *To get a peanut butter coated brown rice crisp filling*, instead of adding marzipan to a hot blend of chocolate and tahini. In a bowl put some rice crisps and roll ½ teaspoon of peanut butter thoroughly and add to the middle of the hot blend as a filling.

- *Replace regular chocolate with sugar free chocolate.*

- *Place Maraschino cherries, raspberry jam, and halva as filling.*

{ Research suggests that eating dark chocolate will aid a healthy heart, assist in weight loss, avoid sugar addiction. Also, tahini is rich in calcium }

Unique Treats

Homemade Almond Milk

~You won't feel tired starting the day with a full cup of energy ~

5 servings
About 65 calories per serving

Ingredients:

1 ½ cups whole raw almonds with the peel
5 cups mineral water (for thicker texture, 4 cups mineral water)
Optional (to sweeten): 4 Medjool pitted dates, 1 tablespoon honey, or any other sweetener

Method:

1.
Soak almonds in regular water for at least two days.
2.
Drain and rinse the almonds.
3.
Using a blender, blend the almonds and mineral water on high speed approximately 2 minutes
4.
Strain and squeeze the almonds using nut milk bag into bowl.
(use remaining almonds for no sugar added sweet vegan bites in secret!)
5.
Blend strained milk with dates, honey, or sweetener in blender.
6.
Refrigerate almond milk.

Mazal's Secrets

- *Creating mouthwatering Vegan Bites: In a small bowl mix everything, 1 ½ cup (remaining) almonds, 15 medjool dates (without pit, washed, and mashed in ½ cup hot water), 2 tablespoons almond butter, and ¾ cup desiccated coconut (optional). To achieve a brown color add 2 tablespoons cocoa powder. Form 1" round ball from batter. Roll ball in coconut. Refrigerate or bake 15 minutes. About 45 servings.*

- *For sesame milk, use the same amount of ingredients (can also mix almonds and sesame)*

- *Create delicious smoothie with the almond milk, just add add banana, strawberries, etc.*

{ Almond milk is an excellent substitute for cow's milk causes swelling And allergies. It is rich in calcium , vitamin D , competitors and contrasting Antioxidant , helps metabolism and facilitates digestion }

Vegan Bites

Unique Treats

112 — 113

Mazal's Secrets

P For Passover option, use equal amount of crushed gluten free matzo (matzah) instead of oatmeal...absolutely amazing!

• Bars can be separated best when cool.

• If bar is too soft bake for additional 5 minutes

Ginger Energy Bar

~This snack is very tasty, energizing, and filling, and may even substitute for breakfast. ~

24 servings
About 216 calories per serving

Ingredients:

2 large eggs
¼ cup canola or olive oil
¾ cup almond butter (organic)
2 teaspoon vanilla extract
½ cup honey
¾ cup dark brown turbinado sugar
2 tablespoons pumpkin seeds
½ cup raisins
¼ cup dried cranberries
1-2 tablespoons ground ginger
½ teaspoon ground cinnamon
A pinch of ground clove
2 tablespoons chia seeds
2 tablespoons flax seeds
¾ cup a mixture of chopped nuts and almonds
4 chopped dried dates
1 teaspoon of baking soda
½ teaspoon baking powder
3 cups of gluten-free oats

Streusel topping:

2 tablespoons dried cranberries
2 tablespoons pumpkin seeds
2 tablespoons of oats

Method:

1.
Preheat oven to 350 degrees F. Place rack in the middle of oven. Line medium oven tray with parchment paper. Spray baking spray lightly.

2.
Using a fork beat the eggs with sugar, honey, oil, baking soda and spices.

3.
Gradually add remaining ingredients to form unified mixture.

4.
Place the mixture on the prepared tray, using a silicone spatula smooth the mixture flat.

5.
Using a knife, score the mixture to create long rectangular shaped bars (like in the picture).

6.
Decorate with streusel topping.

7.
Bake for approximately 10 minutes in preheated oven - go over the lines and keep on baking for about 10 minutes.

8.
Remove from heat and move to rack to cool to firmness for about 2 hours.
Store in refrigerator

Unique Treats

Mazal's Secrets

P For Passover option, use equal amount of crushed gluten-free matzo (matzah) instead of oatmeal...absolutely amazing!

Can add chocolate chips.

Vegan Energy Bars (No-bake)

~Double up, the name says it all, perfect to sneak on a busy day~

24 servings
About 178 calories per serving

Ingredients:

⅔ cup organic honey
1 tablespoon coconut oil
2 teaspoons peanut butter (or almond butter or tahini paste)
1 tablespoon flax seed
2 tablespoons chia seeds
½ teaspoon ginger
½ teaspoon cinnamon
A pinch of sea salt
¼ cup raw pumpkin seeds
4 chopped Medjool dates
4 chopped prunes
3 chopped apricots
¼ cup chopped raw walnuts
1 cup chopped raw almonds
¾ cup dried cranberries or raisins
1½ cup gluten-free oats

Method:

1.
Line a pan with parchment paper.

2.
In a medium skillet, mix honey and coconut oil on medium heat. Add peanut butter and mix well using a big spoon. Turn heat off and add the oats. Mix well.

3.
In a small bowl, mix cinnamon, ginger, salt, flax and chia seeds. Add mixture to the skillet. Continue to add pumpkin seeds, dates, prunes, apricots, walnuts, almonds, and raisins to form unified mixture.

4.
Place mixture on prepared pan. Place another parchment paper on top of mixture, and press well with hands for flatness.

5.
Freeze for 1 hour. Remove parchment paper and cut (square or rectangle shapes).
Store in fridge or freezer.

Unique Treats

Mazal's Secrets

- Can be served cold
- Can be filled with dried fruits such as apricots, figs and pine nuts

Baked Stuffed Apples

A nice alternative to treat yourself on the holidays.

Medium pyrex
5 servings
About 221 calories per serving

Ingredients:

5 medium granny smith apples
3 tablespoons coconut oil
1 tablespoon olive oil
2 tablespoons agave (raspberry jam or maple syrup)
⅓ cup dried cranberries
⅓ cup raisins
1 tablespoon dark brown turbinado sugar
½ cup cinnamon
¼ cup cloves
½ cup chopped almonds or granola
½ cup raspberry or strawberry jam
3 tablespoons freshly squeezed lemon juice

Garnish:

¼ cup fresh pomegranate juice
1 teaspoon agave (or melted raspberry jam)
Seeds from half a pomegranate

Method:

1.

Preheat oven to 350 degrees. Place rack in the middle of oven. In a pyrex serving dish lightly spray baking oil.

2.

Rinse apples. De-core with a peeler, dry and brush inside and out with 1 tablespoon olive oil and 1 tablespoon lemon juice. Place apples on the prepared pyrex.

3.

In a small bowl using a spoon mix 2 tablespoons coconut oil with 2 tablespoons agave, add dry cranberries, raisins, turbinado sugar, cinnamon, cloves, and chopped almonds. Using a spoon, stuff the cored apples.

4.

In a separate small bowl, mix raspberry jam, 1 tablespoon coconut oil and microwave for one second to become more smooth. Add 2 tablespoons lemon juice and mix. Pour the liquid over the stuffed apples, spray each apple with baking oil.

5.

Bake uncovered approximately 50 to 60 minutes.

6.

Mix the garnish: ¼ cup fresh pomegranate juice, 1 teaspoon agave or melted jam and pour over apples. Scatter pomegranate seeds on top.

Serve warm or cold

Unique Treats

Baked Almond Pancake

On mondays, my day off, I enjoy making this guilt free for the family.
4 pancakes = 1 egg + 32 almonds

20 servings
About 105 per serving

Ingredients:

4 large eggs
Pinch of sea salt
1-2 tablespoons honey, maple, or stevia
½ cup Tofutti sour cream or vanilla soy yogurt
1 tablespoon vanilla extract
1 teaspoon baking powder
1 leveled teaspoon baking soda
¼ teaspoon cinnamon
2¼ cups blanched almond flour

Mazal's Secrets

- Can replace Tofutti sour cream with non-dairy yogurt or 1 mashed banana.
- Can add chocolate chips.

Method: Bake version

1.
Preheat oven to 350 degrees F. Place rack in the middle of oven. Lightly spray a large tray (or parchment paper covered tray) with baking oil.

2.
In a medium bowl, using a wire whisk whip eggs with salt, honey, Tofutti sour cream, vanilla, baking powder, baking soda, and cinnamon.

3.
In a separate small bowl, whisk almond flour and add it to the egg mixture. Mix using a tablespoon to form a unified mixture.

4.
Place a tablespoon of mixture on prepared tray, spacing each circle 4" apart. Don't flatten the mixture. Bake for 5 minutes.

5.
Using a pancake turner try to turn pancake, if doesn't release easily bake for another 1-2 minutes. Turn and lightly press with pancake turner. Bake for 2 more minutes or until firm.

6.
Serve with maple syrup, blackberries, sliced banana or any other fruit.

Method: Non-bake version

1.
Lightly spray a large pancake pan with baking oil.

2.
Same as above

3.
Same as above

4.
Place a tablespoon of mixture on prepared pan, spacing each circle 4" apart. Don't flatten the mixture. Cook on medium heat for 5 minutes.

5.
Using a pancake turner try to turn pancake, if doesn't release easily cook for another 1-2 minutes. Gently flip using a pancake turner and press lightly with a pancake turner. Cook for 1-2 minutes or until firm.

6.
Same as above

Makes about 16 pancakes.

Same taste, but different style:
Take the batter, spray the canola on the pan, and flip the pancakes on the pan

Place the batter and bake

4 Pancakes = 1 egg + 32 almonds

❝ Just about everybody loves a good muffin! My recipes will show how you can make delicious muffins for breakfast for a healthy and tasty start to your day or for a nice dessert finish to your evening meal. You will find a wide assortment of tastes and ingredients like: apple, quinoa, flax seeds, carrots, pineapple, bananas and zucchini. Your guests will love them! Now choose your muffin, feel free to use any cake in the book to create a mouthwatering cupcake. ❞

Muffins

Muffins

122 — 123

Apple Muffin

This treat can be frozen, but it is too good to resist once you know you have it!

12 cup muffin tray
12 servings
About 215 calories per serving

Ingredients:

3 large eggs
Pinch of sea salt
1 tablespoon freshly squeezed lemon juice
1 cup turbinado sugar
2 teaspoons honey
1 teaspoon cinnamon
1 tablespoon baking powder
½ teaspoon baking soda
¾ cup medium grated apple or apple sauce
1 green apple (Granny Smith) chopped
1 tablespoon tahini paste or almond butter
¼ cup chopped nuts (walnuts or pecans)
1 cup blanched almond flour
1 tablespoon flax seeds
1 tablespoon chia seeds
½ cup raisins
1 cup quinoa flour or gluten-free all purpose flour

Streusel topping:

1 tablespoon turbinado sugar
2 tablespoons sliced almonds
½ teaspoon cinnamon

Method:

1.
Preheat oven to 350 degrees F. Place oven rack in the middle of oven. Lightly spray a muffin tray with baking oil.

2.
In a medium bowl, using a wire whisk whip eggs with salt, lemon juice, sugar, honey, cinnamon, tahini, and ¾ cup medium grated apple.

3.
In a separate bowl, whisk almond flour, quinoa flour, and baking soda. Add chopped green apple, nuts, flax seeds, chia seeds, and raisins, and add it to the egg mixture. Using a tablespoon form a unified mixture.

4.
Pour mixture into prepared muffin tray. Mix the streusel topping: sugar, sliced almonds, cinnamon, and sprinkle on top.

5.
Bake for approximately 25 minutes or until golden brown. Remove from oven and move to rack to cool.

Mazal's Secrets

- While quinoa has much nutritional value, its taste is very dominant and can be replaced with soy flour, gluten-free oats, tapioca or any other gluten-free flour.

- Can use designed cupcake holders!

Muffins

Flax Seed and Cooked Quinoa Muffin

Perfect to take to work with a cup or herbal tea for an energy filled morning

12 cup muffin tray
12 servings
About 316 calories per serving

Ingredients:

2 large eggs
Pinch of sea salt
1 cup dark brown turbinado sugar
2 tablespoons agave syrup
4 tablespoons olive or coconut oil
1 teaspoon vanilla extract
1½ cups cooked quinoa (prepare prior)
½ cup mixture of flax and chia seeds
¾ cup quinoa flour (gluten-free flour)
1 cup blanched almond flour
1 teaspoon baking soda
1 teaspoon baking powder
2 teaspoons cinnamon
½ cup grated carrot
2 apples grated
½ cup raisins
1 cup chopped mixed nuts

Method:

1.
Preheat oven to 350 degrees F. Place oven rack in the middle of oven. Lightly spray a muffin pan with baking oil.

2.
In a medium bowl, using a wire whisk whip eggs with salt, sugar, agave syrup, oil, grated carrot and apples.

3.
In a separate bowl, whisk quinoa flour, almond flour, vanilla extract, baking powder and baking soda. Add flax seeds, chia seeds, cinnamon, raisins, and chopped nuts. Using a silicone spatula gradually fold the flour mixture to the egg mixture. Add the cooked quinoa and mix to obtain a unified mixture.

4.
Pour mixture into prepared pan. Bake for approximately 25 minutes or until golden brown.

5.
Remove from oven and move to rack to cool.

Mazal's Secrets

- Recommend to soak the quinoa for 10 minutes, rinse, and cook as directed.

Quinoa is a grain of whole grains, and with the highest protein content of all, it's perfect for vegetarians and vegans. It provides all 9 essential amino acids, making it a complete protein and an excellent source of several B Vitamins, along with most of the minerals needed by the human body, including iron and calcium. Quinoa is a gluten-free and cholesterol-free whole grain, and is available as ground flour.

Muffins

Carrot and Pineapple Muffin
Carrot Cake

Take advantage of all the carrots left in your fridge to find your favorite carrot treat, cupcake or loaf!

12 cup muffin tray
9x5" loaf pan
12 servings
Refer to each for calorie count

Ingredients:

3 large eggs
Pinch of sea salt
¼ cup honey
3 tablespoons agave syrup
4 tablespoons olive or canola oil
¾ cup dark brown turbinado sugar
1 teaspoon baking powder
1 teaspoon baking soda
2 tablespoons chia seed
2 teaspoons cinnamon
½ teaspoon vanilla extract
¼ cup ground flax seed
1¼ cup chopped mixed nuts
¼ cup raisins

About 286 calories per serving

For carrot and pineapple muffins:

Mix all the ingredients and add:
2 cups of gluten-free oats or (1¼ cups quinoa flour plus ¾ cup blanched almond flour)
1 cup grated carrot
1 cup chopped fresh pineapple

About 318 calories per serving

For carrot cake or muffins:

Mix all the ingredients and add:
1¼ cups gluten-free all purpose flour
2 cups grated carrot
¾ cup blanched almond flour

Method:

1.
Preheat oven to 350 degrees F. Set rack in the middle of oven. Lightly spray baking oil on a muffin or loaf pan.

2.
In a medium bowl, whisk eggs and add sugar, salt, vanilla extract, chia seeds, flax seeds, honey, agave, oil, raisins, chopped nuts, baking soda, and baking powder. Mix well with a spoon.

3.
Choose either carrot cake or carrot and pineapple muffins and add the remaining ingredients specified by each recipe (muffin or carrot). Mix well to obtain unified batter.

4.
Pour batter into prepared pan. Bake for approximately 25 minutes until golden brown. Remove from oven and move to rack to cool.

Mazal's Secrets

- Carrot cake can be made as a cupcake.
- Don't be frightened by the calorie count for the cakes because they can be exchanged for a meal, are highly nutritious and filling!

Muffins

Banana Muffin

Very tasty muffins exploit the ripe bananas season.
Short preparation time, aroma boggling, who needs more than that?!

12 cup muffin tray
12 servings
About 283 calories per serving

Ingredients:

3 large eggs
Pinch of sea salt
¼ cup turbinado sugar
3 ripe bananas
¼ cup honey
½ cup ground flax seeds
2 cups blanched almond flour
¼ cup chopped walnuts
1 tablespoon of rice flour
½ teaspoon vanilla extract
½ teaspoon baking soda
1 tablespoon baking powder

Garnishment:

¼ cup chocolate chips

Method:

1.
Preheat oven to 350 degrees F. Place oven rack in the middle of oven. Lightly spray a muffin pan with baking oil.

2.
Using a handheld mixer, whip eggs with salt, sugar, honey, and banana.

3.
In a separate small bowl, whisk almond flour, vanilla extract, flax seeds, walnuts, rice flour, baking powder and baking soda. Using a silicone spatula, gradually fold flour mixture into the egg mixture to obtain a unified mixture.

4.
Optional: garnish the muffins with chocolate chips

5.
Pour mixture into prepared pan. Bake for approximately 25 minutes or until golden brown.

6.
Remove from oven and move to rack to cool.

Mazal's Secrets

- Bake the batter in a loaf pan for Banana Bread Substitute blanched almond flour with 1¼ cup of gluten-free flour

Muffins

Zucchini Muffin
{Zucchini Bread}

Rich of health and taste, serve to those you love without spoiling how much love was put into the creation

12 cup muffin tray
9x5" loaf pan
12 servings
About 259 calories per serving

Ingredients:

3 large eggs
Pinch of sea salt
1¼ cup turbinado sugar
¼ cup olive oil or coconut oil
¾ Glass of freshly squeezed orange juice (or soy milk)
¼ teaspoon ground nutmeg
½ teaspoon ground cloves
1 cup of mixed nuts and ground almonds
¼ cup pumpkin seeds
½ cup golden raisins (plus two tablespoons for decoration)
1 ½ dark breed grated zucchini
2 grated apples
1 tablespoon baking powder
¼ cup ground flax seeds
¼ cup chia seeds
1 cup blanched almond flour
1½ cup soy flour or any gluten-free flour

Streusel Topping:

2 tablespoons slivered almonds
2 tablespoon turbinado sugar
½ teaspoon cinnamon
2 tablespoons golden raisins (optional)

Mazal's Secrets

- For zucchini-bread, bake the recipe in a Loaf pan. Avoid the raisins and sugar and replace with 1 tablespoon honey. Also replace apple sauce with ¼ tofutti sour cream.

Method:

1.
Preheat oven to 350 degrees F. Place oven rack in the middle of oven. Lightly spray a muffin pan or zucchini loaf with baking oil.

2.
Using a wire whisk beat the eggs with salt, sugar, oil, and orange juice.

3.
Add nutmeg, cloves, mixed nuts, pumpkin seeds, raisins, zucchini, apples, baking powder, flax/chia seeds, almond flour, and soy flour. Mix to obtain a unified mixture.

4.
Pour mixture into prepared pan.

5.
Mix the streusel topping: almonds, sugar, cinnamon, and raisins and garnish the batter.

6.
Bake in preheated oven approximately 25 minutes until color is light golden brown. Insert toothpick between center and edge comes out clean.

7.
Remove from the oven and move to rack to cool

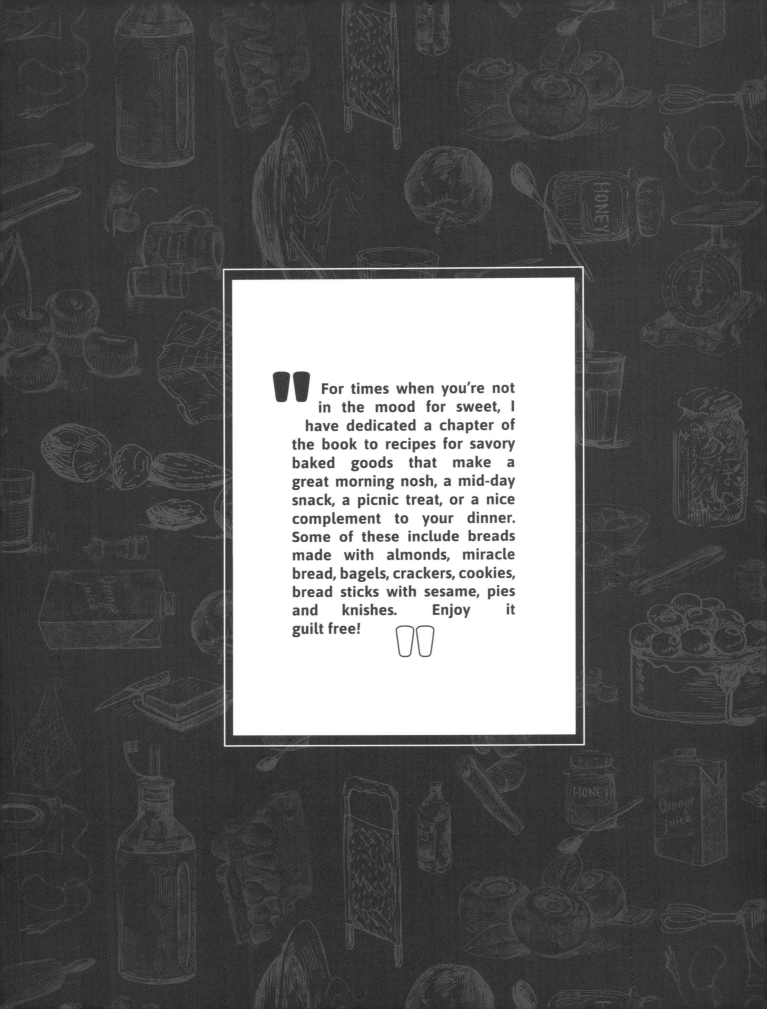

❝ For times when you're not in the mood for sweet, I have dedicated a chapter of the book to recipes for savory baked goods that make a great morning nosh, a mid-day snack, a picnic treat, or a nice complement to your dinner. Some of these include breads made with almonds, miracle bread, bagels, crackers, cookies, bread sticks with sesame, pies and knishes. Enjoy it guilt free! ❞

Savory

Savory Baked Goods

Almond Bread

~I love this bread because it is not carbs even though it tastes like bread, all you need is to add some tofutti cream with vegetable on the side!~

9x5" loaf pan
Muffin pan (for rolls)

12 servings
About 263 calories per serving

Ingredients:

3 large eggs
½ teaspoon sea salt
1 teaspoon baking soda
½ teaspoon honey
⅓ cup tofutti sour cream
1 teaspoon apple cider vinegar
3 tablespoons olive oil
3 ½ cups blanched almond flour

Garnishment:

1 tablespoon olive oil
1 tablespoon sesame seeds
1 tablespoon black sesame seeds or, pumpkin seeds

Method:

1.
Preheat oven to 350 degrees F. Place oven rack in middle of oven. Fit a parchment round cut-to-size into bottom of springform. Spray parchment and sides of springform lightly with cooking spray (or use a muffin pan, without parchment paper, sprayed with cooking spray).

2.
Using a wire whisk beat the eggs and add honey, oil , apple vinegar, tofutti sour cream and salt.

3.
Whisk the almond flour, gradually add to the egg mixture and mix until a smooth batter. Pour into prepared pan.

4.
Brush the top with olive oil and garnish with sesame seed to liking

5.
Bake in preheated oven approximately 50 to 60 minutes until color is light golden brown. Insert toothpick between center and edge comes out clean. Remove from oven and move to rack to cool.

Mazal's Secrets

- Bake the bread with almond meal
- Give up the tofutti sour cream and add another egg to the recipe
- Add any seeds (sunflower, chia, flax seeds, raisins) of liking
- Use dry or fresh rosemary or olives

Savory

Miracle Bread

Start the morning with a healthy sandwich made with almond butter or tahini

12 servings
Refer to each for calorie count

INGREDIENTS:

Two Easy Options
About 116 calories per serving
OPTION 1: (5 easy ingredients)
1 teaspoon baking powder
2 teaspoons honey or maple syrup or stevia
3 teaspoons almond meal flour or blanched almond flour
4 eggs
5 tablespoons almond butter or 100% raw tahini paste
Pinch of sea salt

About 95 calories per serving
OPTION 2:
5 large eggs
7 tablespoons natural almond butter or 100% tahini paste
2 teaspoon honey
1 teaspoon baking powder
Pinch of sea salt

Method:

1.
With a mixer slowly scramble the eggs, and add option 1 or option 2
2.
Decorate top with slivered almonds, pumpkin seeds or sesame seeds.
3.
Bake in loaf pan at 350 degrees for 25-30 minutes.

Mazal's Secrets

- Don't be surprised if the Miracle bread is extremely runny before baking, it'll expand once baked.

- For a sweeter bread, add a tablespoon of honey or maple

- Peanut Butter Miracle Bread (use either option); just substitute almond butter for peanut butter in above recipe.

Almond butter

Tahini

Savory

138 — 139

Mazal's Secrets

- Add chia or caraway seeds to the dough
- Decorate the Pretzel with zatar or a pinch of coarse sea salt.
- Recipe can simultaneously bake 3 pastries of either: pretzels, breadsticks or crackers

Almond Savory Bagels,
Breadsticks and Crackers

2 versions (soft or crispy)

About 24 servings

About 261 calories (3 pretzels without cheese)

Ingredients for soft version:

Pretzels, breadstick and salted crackers

1 large egg
½ teaspoon sea salt
1 tablespoon apple cider vinegar
1 teaspoon honey
1 tablespoon olive oil
1 tablespoon dried thyme
½ teaspoon garlic powder
2 tablespoons chia seeds
2 cups blanched almond flour
½ cup sesame or sunflower seeds
1 cup vegan mozzarella style shreds (optional)

About 168 calories (3 bagels without cheese)

Ingredients for crispy version:

Bagels, breadstick and crispy crackers
1 large egg
1 teaspoon sea salt
¼ cup 100% tahini paste
1 tablespoon honey
1 tablespoon olive oil
2 ½ tablespoons of tofutti cream cheese
1 teaspoon baking powder
½ teaspoon ground caraway seeds or cumin
1 teaspoon chia seeds
1 teaspoon ground flax seeds
1 cup quinoa flour or gluten-free flour
¼ cup blanched almond flour
1 cup vegan mozzarella style shreds (optional)
1 egg yolk mixed with 1 tablespoon of olive oil for decoration

Garnishment: for both recipes

1 cup of sesame or sesame mixture of white and black
1 egg yolk
1 tablespoon of olive oil

Method: Soft or Crispy

1.
In a medium bowl using a fork, mix the egg, honey, oil, and salt.

2.
Add the remaining ingredients from either soft or crispy version until unified dough achieved. (If the dough is still soft add more almond flour).

3.
Allow the dough to rest for 30 minutes.

4.
Set oven to 350 degrees F. Place oven rack in the middle of oven. Line tray with parchment paper and spray baking oil.

5.
Sprinkle a little flour onto work surface to prevent the dough from sticking.

With the dough create circles in the form of pretzels, breadsticks. (optional: create all shapes simultaneously) Move each to prepared tray about 2" apart.

For Pretzels:

For garnishment: mix egg yolk and olive oil and brush pretzels. Spread sesame seeds on pretzel or breadstick (if you want extra then also dip into sesame seeds)

For Crackers: flatten dough on prepared tray equally about ¼ inch thick. Cut the corners to achieve a straight edge, cut dough into square or rectangle shape. For garnishment: mix egg yolk and olive oil and brush crackers. Spread sesame seeds

6.
Bake approximately 15 minutes until golden brown. Let cool out of oven (for crispy: let cool in the oven)

Savory

Vegetable Tofu Quiche

Scrumptious quiche that leaves a lingering taste. Vegetarians can never have enough.

Medium pyrex
10 servings
About 260 calories per serving

Ingredients:

4 large eggs
¼ teaspoon Sea Salt
¼ teaspoon cayenne pepper (or black or white pepper)
¼ teaspoon garlic powder
1 cup cooked banana squash
1 small onion, finely chopped
2 garlic cloves (crushed garlic paste)
1 thinly sliced zucchini
10 sliced mushrooms
12 asparagus cut to medium pieces
1 cup of mixed peppers red, yellow and orange strips
8 oz of tofutti sour cream
8 oz tofutti cream cheese
1 cup vegan mozzarella style shreds
½ cup blanched almond flour

Garnishment:

(over the top of quiche, before baking)
Save some asparagus, mushroom, zucchini, and mixed peppers to decorate the top of the quiche
½ cup vegan mozzarella style shreds

Method: (without the pie base)

1.
In a small skillet cook the banana squash with enough water to cover the squash.

2.
Sautee the onion with light olive oil, then toss with asparagus and add the mushroom (after saute, leave some for garnishment for the top).

3.
In a mixer, beat the whole eggs with spices. Reduce the speed frothing froth add the cooked banana squash, tofutti sour cream, and tofutti cream cheese to get smooth batter.

4.
Next mix gently with a spatula and add the garlic, ½ cup mozzarella, ¼ cup blanched almond flour to the egg mixture. Add the sauteed mixture, zucchini, and mixed peppers (save some for garnishment!) to the egg mixture and gradually obtain a unified mixture.

5.
Set the oven to 350 degrees F. Place oven rack in the middle of oven. Lightly spray baking oil on pyrex and spread ¼ cup almond flour (if using the quiche base avoid almond flour).

6.
Pour the batter into the prepared pyrex and spread the garnishment that is set aside on top.

7.
Bake approximately 45 minutes to 1 hour until golden. Remove from the oven and place on a rack to cool. With a knife go along the edges to avoid quiche sticking to pyrex. Allow it to sit for 1 hour before serving.

Serve warm or cold.

Optional tart crust as the quiche base (quiche in picture baked without tart crust)
1 ½ cups blanched almond flour
½ teaspoon sea salt
½ teaspoon baking soda
¼ cup olive oil or coconut oil
2 tablespoons agave nectar
2 tablespoon sesame seeds or dried thyme (optional)

Method:

1.
Preheat oven to 350 degrees F. Place oven rack in middle of oven. Lightly spray baking oil on 9" serving pyrex.

2.
In a large bowl, combine the blanched almond flour, salt, and baking soda.

3.
In a medium bowl, beat together the olive oil or coconut oil, sesame seeds and agave nectar. Stir the wet ingredients. Gradually add the almond flour mixture to the wet ingredients until thoroughly combined. Press the dough into and along the sides of prepared pyrex.

4.
Bake approximately 7 to 10 minutes, until golden. Remove from the oven and let cool before filling.

5.
After filling, bake approximately 50 minutes until golden.

Mazal's Secrets

- For a dairy recipe, substitute equivalent amounts of dairy for soy
- Cool for a few hours before cutting.
- Perfect for when it's cold
- Can use the quiche base to make savory biscuits. Roll the quiche base into a long loaf, freeze it, then cut the frozen loaf into thin slices, and place it on wax paper that is sprayed with canola oil and place it right away into the preheated 350 degree oven until golden.